JOHN

Discovering
Battlefields
of England

SHIRE PUBLICATIONS LTD

ACKNOWLEDGEMENTS

The author acknowledges with gratitude the help received from many people whose local knowledge he has drawn upon, and in particular to R. G. Willis, M.A., and A. J. Brown, M.A., for information on Maldon; Charles Torlesse, A.C.A., who guided him round Yorkshire's many battlefields; James Roe of Preston Historical Society; Miss D. M. Hudson, F.L.A., who supplied information on The Standard; and Major Naesmyth of Posso, R.A., who accompanied him on numerous battlefield excursions and whose compass was invaluable.

Works of reference to which the author is indebted include Lt. Col. A. H. Burne's *English Battlefields* and *More English Battlefields* (Methuen), Paul Kendall's *Richard III* and *Warwick the Kingmaker* (Allen and Unwin), Clarendon's *History of the Great Rebellion* (Folio Society), and Price's *Guide to Leominster* (1795).

The battle plans were drawn by Shirley Barker. The cover photograph of Richards III's standard on the Bosworth Battlefield trail is by Cadbury Lamb. The plates in the text are acknowledged as follows: John Kinross 8, 34, 36 and 37; the Tate Gallery, London, 42; all others by Cadbury Lamb.

Owing to the threat to Naseby with the new A1/M1 link road and to save further battlefields from development – Blore Heath is already threatened by a new quarry – the Battlefields Trust has been established. For details of membership apply to: Kelvin van Hasselt, 2 Winton Close, Solvent Avenue, Lymington, Hampshire SO41 9SU.

Printed in Great Britain by CIT Printing Services, Press Buildings, Merlins Bridge, Haverfordwest, Dyfed SA61 1XF.

CONTENTS

3

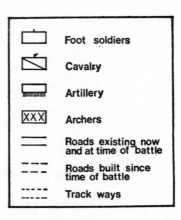

Key to the symbols used in the battle plans.

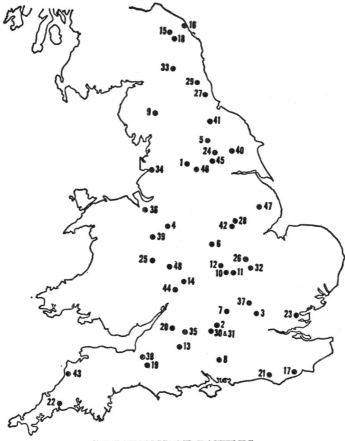

LOCATIONS OF BATTLES

ASHDOWN, 8th January, 871

Berkshire O/S Landranger 174 (535 820)

The importance of the battle of Ashdown, which took place in a year of battles, lies mainly in the fact that it was the only one of six in which the Danes were beaten by the Wessex Anglo-Saxons, and that details of it have come down to us from an account by Bishop Asser of Sherborne, a friend of Alfred.

King Ethelred of Wessex (not to be confused with the 'Unready' who ruled a hundred years later) and his brother Alfred, later 'the Great', were surprised in 870 by the sudden seizure of Reading by the Danes under their two kings, Bagsac and Halfden. The Danish foraging party was defeated at Englefield but a direct attack on Reading failed and Ethelred retreated along the old Ridgeway, an extension of the Icknield Way running across the top of the Berkshire Downs from Streatley to Marlborough. In the winter of 870-871 this track was dry and hard, while the valley roads were wet. Thus an army could move quickly only on the high ground. Bagsac soon realised this and advanced on Ethelred, who was awaiting more troops at Lowbury Hill about two miles north-east of the present village of Compton and four miles west of Goring. On the morning of 8th January, Ethelred saw the Danish banners advancing towards him, with Bagsac on one side of the Ridgeway and the Danish Earls on the other. He divided his army to meet them but did not move. Being a religious king he chose this moment to order his half of the army down on their knees to pray for a swift victory. Alfred looked on in horror, and according to Bishop Asser, "he had to choose between withdrawing altogether or beginning the battle without waiting for his brother". Before losing the advantage of high ground, "like a wild boar" he charged on the banners of the Earls, who retreated to a small hill with a thorn tree, called Nachedorm, or the naked thorn, later in the Domesday Book.

Five of the Earls were killed, and the Danes fled back to their camp at Reading. Ethelred's attack later was just as successful and King Bagsac was killed, Halfden escaping with the remainder to Reading. Two weeks later they were in the field again, but the Anglo-Saxons were no longer afraid. They had defeated the invaders for the first time and Alfred obtained a period of peace in Wessex until Ethandun seven years later completed his victory.

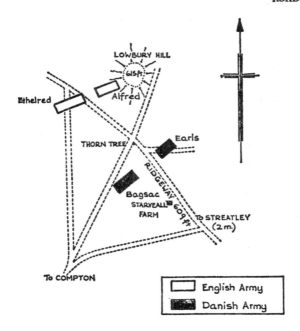

Battle of Ashdown, 871

Ashdown today:

Take A329 from Reading to Streatley, turn left on B4009 to Aldworth. Turn right and follow a sign 'To the Downs'. The exact position of this battle is not known for certain but the most likely position, after the Saxons had retreated from Reading and assuming they had covered ten miles, would be on the old Ridgeway road from Goring towards Wantage which was one of Alfred's headquarters. Lowbury Hill, which is just on the right of the cross tracks after the farm, is the highest point on Alfred's route and Starveall Farm, where the Danes camped before the battle, lies below it commanding a good position of the Saxon camp. There are thorn bushes around and although the place called Nachedorm is difficult to position, it is most likely to have been in the centre of the battlefield.

7

ETHANDUN, 878

Wiltshire O/S Landranger 184 (933 523)

In the year 871 England seemed a doomed kingdom. Northumbria was occupied by the Norsemen, Mercia was divided between Danes and Anglo-Saxons and only Wessex, or that part of it west of Southampton Water, retained under King Ethelred a semblance of order and resistance against the invaders. By the close of the year Ethelred had died and his brother Alfred took over the kingdom. The latter had proved his worth as a soldier at Ashdown and the Danish King Guthrum left him alone for five years, until 877 when Exeter was seized by a Danish raiding party from Wareham. Alfred moved to Chippenham where he held a great feast in celebration of Twelfth Night. The sentries relaxed or the storm concealed Guthrum's advancing men, but in the swift battle that followed Alfred was lucky to escape with a few thegns to Athelney, his hideout on the river Parrett, not far from Sedgemoor.

For two months he gathered fresh troops, sending out messengers to Hampshire and Wiltshire for the local fyrds or militias to meet him in May at Brixton Deverill, between Shaftesbury and Warminster. It was a well-known spot as Ecgbryghts-stane, a standing stone near there, was often used as a meeting place. From here Alfred marched to Eastleigh Wood by the river Wylye and, collecting the Hampshire men, he turned north towards Chippenham. The Battle of Ethandun or Bratton Down took place on open downland, but Alfred was careful to retain the heights and it was Guthrum's army that had to march out of Chippenham for ten miles and climb up over the down to get at Alfred. The Danes had lost their famous Raven banner, a silk flag that brought them victory in battle, in an unsuccessful attack a few months earlier against a Saxon strongpoint on Exmoor, and superstition played its part. For hours men fought with sword and axe. According to the Anglo-Saxon Chronicle, Alfred "put them to flight, pursued them as far as their camp and there sat down fourteen days".

The Peace of Wedmore followed. Guthrum and thirty of his men came to meet Alfred near Athelney, where a great baptismal ceremony was held and the heathens were converted, mercy being shown to the vanquished. According to legend, the Westbury White Horse on Bratton Down was carved by Alfred's soldiers to commemorate the battle. As a

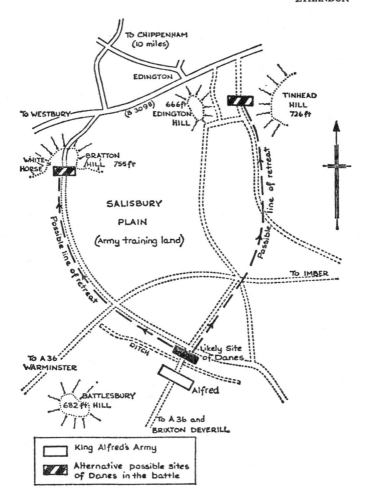

Battle of Ethandun, 878

result there were fourteen years of peace and England was divided into two zones by a border that roughly followed the present A5. Although there were further battles, the threat to Wessex passed and in the following century the Danes came to England more as settlers than as pirates.

Ethandun today:

Take the Marlborough-Westbury road (B3098) and the villages of Edington and Bratton are next to each other. Bratton Castle has ditches of 15 to 20 feet in depth and would be an ideal defensive position. There is a ditch above Warminster similar to the Wansdyke (marked Ancient Ditch on map 167) which may well be the Danes' first position. Most of Salisbury Plain is W.D. property and guns are now firing over Alfred's battlefield.

MALDON, 11th August, 991

Essex O/S Landranger 168 (865 055)

For over a hundred years after Alfred the Danes did not succeed in winning a large battle. Their raiding parties were beaten off or were not of sufficient strength to make any headway. In 991, during the reign of Ethelred the Unready, the son of King Edgar, an organised army of Danes and Norwegians descended on Ipswich, which they sacked, and, carrying off arms and supplies, the raiders sailed south to the river Blackwater where they made their headquarters on Northey Island, about a mile from Maldon.

An epic poem describing the battle has survived. The English leader was Britnoth, a giant of 6 feet 9 inches who was over 60 but still a forceful general. He collected an army which, though small in number, was experienced in battle. Three men guarded the narrow causeway to Northey Island and until the high tide had ebbed the Danes were powerless to move. Their leader asked for tribute to be paid, but Britnoth was determined to fight. "Here stands an earl not mean (small in stature) with this company . . . not so lightly shall you come by treasure," he said.

According to tradition he stepped back and allowed the Danes across the river, but more likely they swarmed over the causeway or crossed in boats and descended on the English. Their archers beat back Britnoth's men and, forming themselves into a wedge formation, they charged. Fighting mostly with spears and swords the English were overwhelmed, Britnoth was killed and his head cut off by the Danish leader.

Half the English fled, but the three heroes who had held the causeway surrounded Britnoth's body and joined by a few

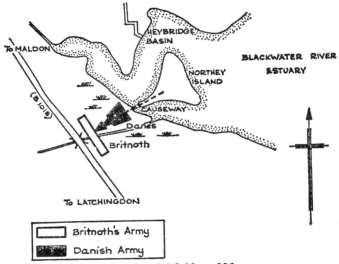

Battle of Maldon, 991

more they fought on until overwhelmed and killed. The Danes had no more strength left to follow up their victory but Maldon was the beginning of the Danegeld and Ethelred was forced to pay 10,000 pounds silver in tribute money. The Danes had come to stay and England was forced to pay for them until 1016 when the Danish king Canute became king of England.

Men have forgotten Britnoth but in 1769 a tall skeleton was found in Ely Cathedral. In place of the head was a lump of wax, and from head to feet it was 6 feet 9 inches.

Maldon today:
From Chelmsford take the A414 to Maldon. The battlefield is about half a mile down the B1018 to Latchingdon. The causeway is marked on Stanford's Chart of the Essex Rivers as a 'road at low water'. It is about 12 feet wide and 170 yards long. The Blackwater river tide approaches it from both sides and if you step off it you sink up to your knees in black slime. No wonder the Danes waited until low water before attacking and it is probable that their ships were too far away as the wharf on Northey Island is further round facing Heybridge Basin. There is no monument.

On the death of Edward the Confessor in January 1066, his successor Harold was beset with difficulties. His claim to the throne was challenged by William, Duke of Normandy, who was a cousin of Edward's whereas Harold was only a brother-in-law. In May Harold's rebellious brother Tostig, the exiled Earl of Northumberland, was in arms against him and in September the King of Norway, Harold Hardrada, suddenly joined forces with Tostig and set sail from his base at Bergen for the Humber estuary.

Harold was watching the south coast with his levies, but early in September he disbanded them and went to London with his house carls. In York the Earl of Mercia, Edwin, and his brother Morcar were defeated by Hardrada and his Vikings at Fulford, a few miles south of the city. The invaders had left their ships at Riccall on the Ouse, having sailed up from the Humber. Instead of advancing on defenceless York they returned to their base, perhaps because Hardrada was concerned about his son Olaf, who was in charge of the boats. Harold had set out from London for the north as soon as he had been able to collect an army. Arriving at Tadcaster on 24th September, he entered York the following day. His men were tired, but Harold was strengthened by Edwin and Morcar's remaining troops. The enemy were resting at Stamford on the Derwent river, where arrangements had been made to exchange prisoners. Harold had no intention of resting while his enemy were unprepared for an attack. The English, numbering about 4,000, attacked the invaders who were numerically superior, perhaps 5,000, but they had left Olaf with a strong force at Riccall twelve miles away.

The Vikings were on both sides of the Derwent, which is about 40 feet wide, and the bridge was 500 yards upstream from the present bridge. It was built of wooden poles and must have been very narrow. The English charged down to the river bank, where many of the Norsemen were positioned. The enemy were without their heavy armour which had been left behind at Riccall, and they reeled back in surprise. Hardrada gave the order to retreat to the Battle Flats, a level piece of ground 50 feet above the river to the east. According to legend a giant Norseman held the bridge with his axe for at least half an hour while Tostig and

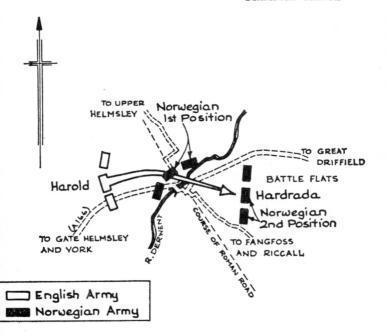

Battle of Stamford Bridge, 1066

Hardrada marshalled their troops and sent a messenger to Olaf for reinforcements. An English soldier found a swill barrel which he emptied and used as a boat to get under the bridge without being seen. With his long spear he thrust between the poles of the bridge floor at the brave Norseman, and wounded him. Harold then led his men over the river and the main battle began.

Deceived by a feigned withdrawal, the Norsemen, who had formed a shield wall, advanced upon the English and a bloody struggle took place. Hardrada was hit in the throat by an arrow and Tostig took over the command. In a brief pause Harold offered his brother his life if he withdrew, but Tostig was playing for time until his reinforcements arrived. The road to Stamford from Riccall is not a comfortable march for heavily armed warriors and having to fight at once on arrival was too much for them. The English put them to flight. Only a few escaped to their boats, among them Olaf who was forced to promise never to attack England again and allowed to sail away with the survivors. Harold had won a great victory but at some cost, for his army had now to return to a greater foe in the south. On 28th September William landed at Pevensey with a mightier army, determined to capture the English throne.

Stamford Bridge today:

A few miles west of York on A166 the road climbs to the village of Gate Helmsley then descends suddenly to the river Derwent and Stamford Bridge. The old bridge was about 400 yards further upstream, just below the present weir. Today the river is crowded with caravans on one side and traffic on the other. The old mill, however, is being repaired and the memorial stone to the battle is on the small green adjacent to the mill. It has both a simple English inscription and a Norwegian one:— SLAGET VED STAMFORD BRUBLE UTKJEMPET IDISSE TRAKTER DEN 25 SEPTEMBER 1066 (The Battle of Stamford Bridge was fought in this neighbourhood on September 25th 1066).

HASTINGS, 14th October, 1066

Sussex O/S Landranger 199 (746 152)

On 25th September 1066 King Harold won the battle of Stamford Bridge, defeating the Viking raiders who had landed under their leader Harold Hardrada on a plundering expedition. The same day, as if he was in radio contact, William of Normandy and 10,000 men set sail from St. Valery to land two days later at Pevensey. William had met Harold before and had forced him to promise to support William's claim to the throne, which was probably stronger than Harold's as William was a cousin of Edward the Confessor and his great-aunt Emma had married Canute. The nearest claimant was Edgar, grandson of Edmund Ironside and great-grandson of Ethelred the Unready, but as he was a boy the Witan had chosen Harold, Edward's brother-in-law.

The Norman army spent two weeks at Pevensey which they fortified, not daring to venture far inland before Harold, who had stopped in London to gather fresh troops, appeared on the scene. A rendezvous was planned in the Weald Forest but many failed to find it, so when the Saxon army lined the

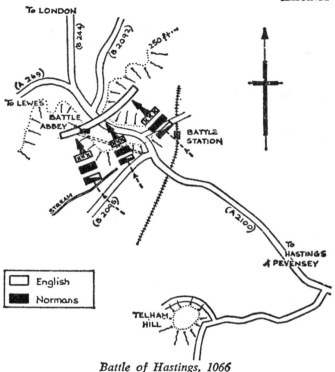

Battle of Hastings, 1066

ridge of Senlac Hill on the London-Hastings road it was probably fewer in number than the Normans. All through the battle, however, new recruits arrived to take the places of the fallen. The house carls, Harold's best troops, fought with long-handled axes and spears. Their shields were long and narrow and formed a defensive wall against arrows. The levies fought with any arms they could find—clubs, stones, knives —and some had shields and bows and arrows.

William's knights were dressed in chain-mail and rode small horses. They were armed with spears and swords and were trained to charge on the flank. When the Norman host approached the long line of Saxons it split into three groups, the Bretons on the left, William in the centre and the Flemings on the right. The archers, armed with short bows, came on

15

ahead followed by the infantry and lastly the knights. At first the arrows did no damage and the Bretons' charge was driven back by Harold's right wing. All day the shield wall held and William had to halt to decide on a new plan. His archers had run out of arrows, but messengers had been sent to Pevensey for more. These were fired high and into the back ranks of Harold's army, one of them wounding Harold in the eye. At the same time there was a combined attack from horsemen and foot soldiers. The shield wall broke, the levies fled and Harold was hacked to death. This part of the hill is now marked by the high altar of Battle Abbey.

Hastings today:

Leave Hastings town by A2100 to Battle which is four miles north-west. The Abbey, which is open to the public, is on the left and the altar marks the spot where Harold fell. The Normans charged from Telham Hill across the B2095 to the ridge on which the Abbey stands. Also on this road is a farmtrack that follows the original Hastings road northwards and provides a good viewpoint. There are more trees than there were in 1066 and the ground level has risen so much that no relics have been found other than an axehead in Marley Lane. There is an audio-visual display in Battle Abbey grounds.

THE STANDARD, NORTHALLERTON, 22nd August, 1138

Yorkshire O/S Landranger 99 (362 981)

King Stephen inherited a troubled kingdom in 1135. The Empress Matilda, like Stephen a grandchild of William I, had an equal claim to the throne, being the daughter of Henry I, and she was supported by King David I of Scotland who had sworn an oath in 1127 to make her Queen of England. He also claimed part of Northumberland as his wife's property and on these two counts led his army of wild Galloway men, pony-mounted cavalry and a few archers to Carlisle, which he soon captured. Moving south-east, he occupied Darlington. King Stephen meanwhile was busy in the south where Robert, Earl of Gloucester, was in revolt at Bristol, and Maminet, Constable of Dover, held Dover for the Earl. Beset on all sides, Stephen had but one faithful ally—the Church. His brother was the Bishop of Winchester and the Archbishop of York was a good friend.

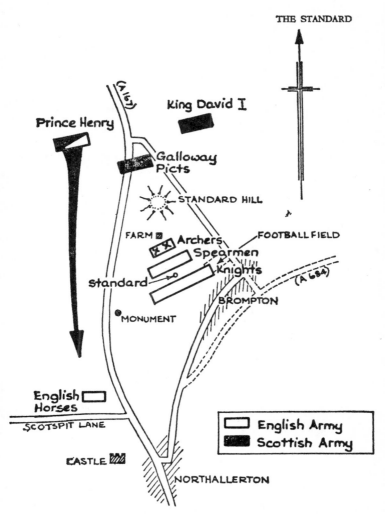

THE STANDARD

King David I

Prince Henry

Galloway Picts

STANDARD HILL

FARM

Archers

FOOTBALL FIELD

Spearmen

Knights

Standard

(A 684)

BROMPTON

MONUMENT

English Horses

SCOTSPIT LANE

☐ English Army
■ Scottish Army

CASTLE

NORTHALLERTON

Battle of The Standard, 1138

When the women of Hexham were taken by the invading Scots to slavery bound together by ropes, Archbishop Thurstan of York organised a holy war against the pagan

Scots. Men flocked to his enormous standard—a ship's mast topped by a silver pyx containing a consecrated wafer and hung with the banners of St. Peter of York, St. John of Beverley and St. Wilfred of Ripon. Two of the English army, Bruce and Balliol, who owned land in Scotland, tried to arrange a truce and offered to help the young Prince Henry of Scotland obtain the Earldom of Northumberland. It was useless. The two armies, each numbering about 12,000 men, with the Scots possibly the larger force, met on Cowton Moor north of Northallerton (where at that time there stood a Norman castle) at six in the morning. The English fought in three lines, the archers in the front, the spearmen next and the men-at-arms and knights in the third line. A mile or so behind the English line were their horses and in the centre of their middle line the mighty standard stood in an open cart.

The Scots were in three groups with the King on the left, Prince Henry and his mounted cavalry on the right, and in front at their own request the wild Picts from Galloway. "Like a hedgehog with its quills", wrote Ailred of Rievaulx, "you might see a Gallwegian bristling with arrows yet still holding his sword." The Scots' wild charge was checked by the English archers and the well-disciplined foot soldiers who moved forward to cover the archers as they collected fresh arrows. Prince Henry, seeing the plight of the Galloway men, led a charge round the English left wing and attacked the English horses, the attendant pages and the rearguard. The situation was saved by the English third line which turned about and encircled the Prince. A mighty struggle took place in which the Danes and Normans in the Scottish army fought so fiercely that the retreating King was joined by Prince Henry and escaped to Carlisle without any effective interruption. Old Thurstan and his second-in-command, Walter Espec of Helmsley, were victorious. The bodies of at least 10,000 were buried in Scotspit Lane. Most of them were Scots. Peace came to Yorkshire but the battle marked the beginning of King Stephen's civil war, not the end.

The Standard today:

Leaving Northallerton by the A167, the monument to the battle stands by the right-hand side of the road about three miles to the north. It has an interesting shield depicting the standard mounted on a cart with the banners of the three bishops. There is a Maltese cross at the top representing the Archbishop. The only flags that fly on the battlefield today are the cornerflags of a football pitch and there are two farms marking the Scots and English positions.

LEWES, 14th May, 1264

Sussex O/S Landranger 198 (396 112)

When Henry III came to the throne in 1216 at the age of nine he inherited a troubled nation from his father King John. During the Regency the Barons regained their power and a new figure emerged—Simon de Montfort, Earl of Leicester, who championed the cause of the new knights and gentry, the poor clergy and the more liberally minded Barons against the King. There followed a struggle for the right to control the government of the country and it was at Lewes that the English Parliament was born.

In 1264 de Montfort gathered a small army of about 4,500 infantry and 500 cavalry and after leaving London made for Lewes where the King and his son Edward, later King

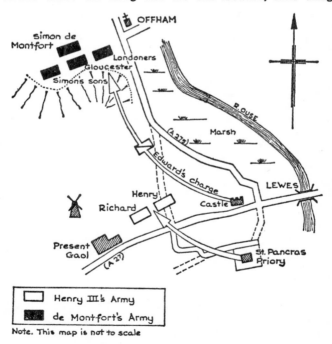

Battle of Lewes, 1264

Edward I, the 'Hammer of the Scots', waited with an army twice the size. Between Offham and Lewes, near the present racecourse, Simon placed his army with Henry and Guy, two of his sons, commanding the right, the Earl of Gloucester the centre, the Londoners on the left and his own experienced troops in reserve. On 14th May the King was quartered in St. Pancras Priory at Lewes and Edward with the cavalry was in Lewes Castle. Nearly a mile away Simon stood ready, anxious to hold the high ground. The Royal cavalry charged the left wing and the Londoners fled taking Prince Edward's force off the field in pursuit for two hours. (There was a similar situation at the Battle of Edgehill in 1642.) When the King and his brother Richard attacked, the forces were more even. "The King was much beaten with swords and maces," reads a contemporary account, "two horses were killed under him and he escaped with difficulty."

Edward returned and captured Simon's abandoned litter or chariot, killing some hostages by mistake and capturing numerous standards. He soon realised that the King had been defeated in his absence and he retired to confront his father at the Priory, losing most of his men on the way. The unfortunate Richard, known as 'The Roman' because he had stood as a candidate in Rome for the Imperial throne, was cut off from the King's forces and was captured in a windmill nearby.

Peace was made at the Mise of Lewes and Henry was kept under guard for fifteen months while Simon set up a Parliament consisting of knights from the shires and two representatives from each of the chartered boroughs. Simon had succeeded where Essex at Edgehill failed nearly four hundred years later. He kept his position and used his forces to defeat his enemy piece by piece with a seasoned reserve as the final shattering blow.

Lewes today:

Take the A27 from Brighton to Lewes and turn left before really entering Lewes on to the A275 to Offham. If you walk up the track on the other side of the road from Offham church you come to Harry's Hill. Simon's position was in between some chalk pits on the left and Lewes racecourse grandstand on the right. He could see the King's approach from the Priory but Lewes Gaol blocks the view today. There is little left of the eleventh-century Lewes Castle except the entrance gateway and keep walls, from one of which one can see the battlefield. A monument in the shape of a knight's helmet stands in St Pancras Priory grounds.

After Lewes, Simon de Montfort looked for allies in Wales and found one in a local patriot, Llewellyn, whose Welsh territory he recognised. By doing this he made many enemies—one of whom, Gilbert de Clare, Earl of Gloucester, raised a force of horsemen in the Welsh Marches. This small army suddenly became important when Prince Edward, still a prisoner of de Montfort, escaped in a hunting party and

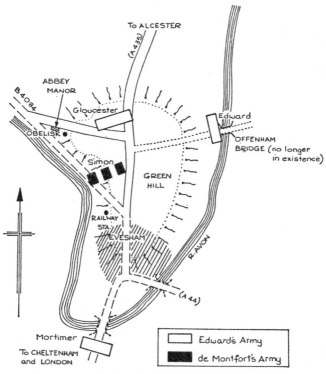

Battle of Evesham, 1265

joined Gloucester in May 1265.

One of Simon's sons, also called Simon, was in Kenilworth with a small force and when later in the summer Edward's army appeared at Worcester, de Montfort set out from Hereford in order to join his son at Kenilworth. On 3rd August he reached Evesham, camping at a bend in the river. Early the following morning a barber on the church tower spotted the banners of the younger Simon advancing from Alcester. Another force was crossing Offenham bridge. Another under Mortimer blocked the bridge on the London road. It took Simon a few minutes to realise he was surrounded and that disaster had overtaken his son. By a brilliant long march two days earlier Edward had surprised young Simon at Kenilworth. He then turned around to march on Evesham and divided his army into three groups to block de Montfort's escape routes, using captured banners to deceive him.

Simon's army was about 5,000 and Edward's and Gloucester's forces amounted to twice the size. "May God have mercy on our souls," said de Montfort when he learnt this, "for our bodies are theirs." With a bold decision he arranged his army in a tight group, the few horsemen in front, the English foot next and the Welsh foot in the rear. There was a heavy downpour and it was a dark morning; with luck Simon might slip between Edward and Gloucester and escape towards Alcester.

Perched on Green Hill Edward could see the enemy's position in spite of the weather. His line recoiled under Simon's charge but the extended wings surrounded the smaller army. Many of the Welsh swam the river and escaped but Simon and most of the English foot were killed where they stood.

Kenilworth Castle held out for many months for de Montfort's cause. King Henry III, who had been Simon's captive, and was nearly killed by Prince Edward's men at Evesham, pursued a policy of moderation. When Edward came to the throne he carried on Simon's political ideas. Parliament grew in strength, the common law was respected, justice prevailed.

Evesham today:

Of all battle monuments, Evesham is probably the hardest to find. Coming into Evesham from Stratford or Alcester turn right on B4084 towards Worcester. Fifty yards further on are the iron gates to Abbey Manor. The obelisk is in the garden, hidden behind a lily pond. This *overlooks* the site of the battle and is inscribed with the following inscription: "On this spot in the reign of Henry III the Battle of

Evesham was fought August IV, 1265 between the King's forces commanded by his eldest son Prince Edward and the Barons under Simon de Montfort, Earl of Leicester, in which the Prince, by his skilled valour, obtained a complete victory." There is a picture of the King's narrow escape from death on the other side. Many of the Welsh were killed at Dead Man's Ait, a meadow opposite the Bridge Inn at Offenham. The stone bridge was demolished in Victorian times. The De Montfort room in the local museum should not be missed. There is a recent tomb to Simon in the churchyard next to the museum.

BOROUGHBRIDGE, 16th March, 1322

Yorkshire O/S Landranger 99 (394 671)

After Bannockburn the English crown was constantly threatened not only by the Scots but by the rebellious barons. Edward II's favourite Piers Gaveston was executed by Warwick and Lancaster, but the king found new favourites in Hugh Despenser and his son, and the latter was soon as unpopular in the Welsh Marches as Gaveston had been in the country as a whole. At the Parliament that met in 1321 the two Despensers were banished and the barons pardoned themselves for acting against the favourites. Edward now looked for any chance to get his revenge. When the Queen was refused admission to Leeds Castle in Kent, he collected an army of Londoners and attacked the castle, which held out for two weeks. When it fell he imprisoned Lady Badlesmere, the owner, and hanged the garrison.

Civil war broke out and Edward marched on Bridgnorth, where Mortimer was gathering an army of rebels. Mortimer was soon defeated and Lancaster, who had raised a strong force in Yorkshire which included the rebel Lords Mowbray, Clifford, Amory and Hereford, set out to Tickhill, near Doncaster, where he besieged the royal castle. The garrison held out and as the King's troops advanced from Cirencester, Lancaster checked them at Burton-on-Trent but Edward crossed the river higher up and pursued the rebels back to Yorkshire. The vanguard of the Earls of Surrey and Kent captured the rebel-held castles of Tutbury and Kenilworth. Lancaster's only hope was to join forces with the Scots and on 16th March 1322 his army reached the river Ure at Boroughbridge.

Meanwhile Sir Andrew Harcla, Edward's warden of

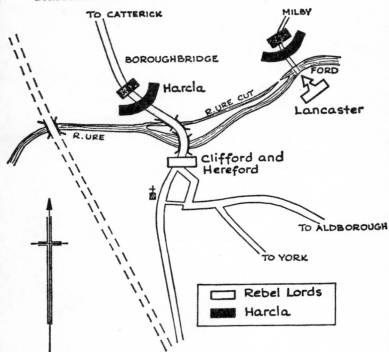

Battle of Boroughbridge, 1322

Carlisle, had come south with his spearmen and archers. Hearing from a spy that the rebels were making for Boroughbridge, he placed his army in two schiltrons on the north bank, putting archers behind the spearmen so that one group could fire easily at the bridge, and the other could defend nearby Milby ford. Lancaster, who had no quarrel with Harcla, tried to reason with him and, when this failed, exclaimed that the knight "would sorely repent and should die a shameful death ere another year should expire".

Lancaster led his horsemen at the ford while Clifford and Hereford dismounted and attacked the bridge. The struggle was fierce but, perhaps remembering Stamford Bridge, one of the Welsh spearmen killed Hereford by thrusting at him from under the bridge. Clifford was wounded and Lancaster

24

could not force the ford. Calling off the remainder of his men, many of whom had deserted, he made a truce with Harcla and camped in the town for the night. Next day Sir Simon de Ward brought 500 men to assist Harcla and Lancaster, with a few remaining followers, was forced into the church. Many of the knights escaped dressed as peasants but Lancaster was captured and led to his own castle of Pontefract where Edward and Earl Despenser held a mock trial and "riding a sorry nag" the "mightiest Earl in Christendom" was led out to his execution. The following year Bruce attacked Edward's army at Byland and routed them. Harcla made his own peace and the Earl of Lancaster's prophesy came true. The victor of Boroughbridge was accused of treachery, tried, hanged, drawn and quartered.

Boroughbridge today:

The town is twenty miles north-west of York on A1. The river is about twenty feet wide. There is a monument to the battle which formerly stood in the main street but was moved some years ago to the neighbouring village of Aldborough.

HALIDON HILL, 19th July, 1333
Northumberland O/S Landranger 75 (972 548)

When Edward III came to the throne in 1330 he was soon to face as much trouble from Scotland as his father. Edward Balliol, a Scot with an equal claim to the Scottish throne as he was a cousin of the Bruces, took an expedition to Fife by sea and defeated the Scots at Duppin Moor. In September 1332 Balliol was crowned at Scone but within a year the combined forces of the Earl of Moray and Archibald Douglas had driven him into the border country. Edward III gathered an army and, declaring void the Treaty of Northampton, which had agreed to recognise the sovereignty of Scotland, joined up with Balliol to besiege the walled town of Berwick-on-Tweed.

Worn down by Edward's great siege engines, the defenders of Berwick agreed in June to surrender the town by 11th July if they were not relieved before that date. It was a situation similar to that of Stirling castle before Bannockburn. The Scottish relieving force managed to cross the Tweed upstream and burn Tweedmouth. In the diversion two hundred of them reached Berwick and the rest pushed on towards Bamburgh.

A new agreement was made between the town and Edward that he would return the hostages by 20th July if two hundred more Scots succeeded in getting through his lines. Douglas led his men back over the river to Duns and Edward, whose army consisted of "murderers, robbers and poachers", posted them on the top of Halidon Hill where he could overlook both the town and the direction from which Douglas would attack. Arranged in three divisions with archers on each wing, the left was commanded by Balliol, the centre by the King and the right wing by Sir Edward Bohun, the Constable.

On 19th July the Scots approached from Duns. They were a larger army than Edward's, which had suffered from desertions, and were arranged also in three divisions under Moray, Robert the Steward and Archibald Douglas. Two hundred picked men commanded by the Earl of Ross were in the rear. Waiting until the first wave of Scots were on the bog before Halidon, Edward's archers opened a devastating fire. Balliol's dismounted knights disposed of the few who reached them and the archers took a heavy toll of the second and third waves. Only Ross stood his ground and fought a rearguard action while the young Robert escaped. The English knights remounted and chased the Scots back to Duns, few of the latter being mounted as their horses had been seized by the frightened Scottish grooms who had watched from Witches Knowle Hill their masters being defeated. Seventy Scottish lords, including Douglas, five hundred knights and several thousand foot soldiers were killed for the loss of one English knight, one man at arms and the Newcastle contingent which had arrived late and was cut down to a man.

Bannockburn had been revenged but Scotland was still undefeated and Balliol, although restored, was never accepted by the Scots, who smuggled their young King David II to safety in France.

Halidon Hill today:

Take the A6105 out of Berwick towards Duns. Turn right at the Maternity Home and then left down an unmade road at the signpost pointing to the battle site. There is no monument but a rough cairn marks the spot and an ordnance survey pointer stands on the crest of the hill. It is a commanding position worth visiting for the magnificent view in all directions.

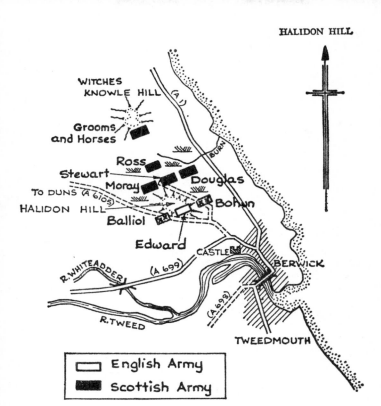

Battle of Halidon Hill, 1333

NEVILLE'S CROSS, 17th October, 1346
Co. Durham O/S Landranger 88 (261 420)

In August 1346 Edward III led his army in France to a great victory over Philip of France at Crecy. The French king in despair called on his ally David II of Scotland to invade England and give him a respite. The English army in the north was commanded by the Archbishop of York, Lord Neville of Raby and Henry, Lord Percy. At a summons to arms at Bishop Auckland an army of at least 15,000 men

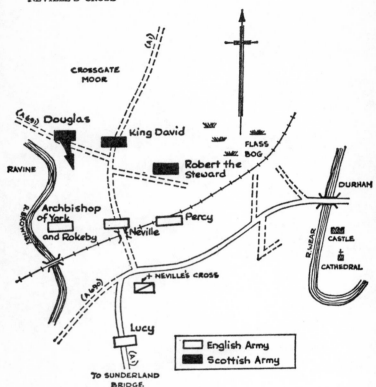

Battle of Neville's Cross, 1346

was assembled, which moved north to attack the Scots, somewhat superior in numbers, who were camped at Bearpark in
Durham.

Surprising the Scottish vanguard at Sunderland Bridge,
Neville, who was in command, led his army on to Red Hill.
On the left was the Archbishop and Sir Thomas Rokeby
and on the right Lord Percy. Each division had a small troop
of archers out in front. The Scots were also in three divisions
commanded by Douglas, King David and Robert the Steward.
Because of the broken nature of the ground and a deep ravine

28

on Douglas's wing they could not face parallel to Neville's army. The initial attack was made by the Scots and when Douglas wheeled to the left to avoid the ravine he mixed with the King's men and the English archers killed many of the Scots by firing into the dense mass of soldiers. Robert the Steward and the rest of the King's forces had some success when they charged and Neville and Percy were pushed back. The crucial moment had come and the English horsemen in the rear were ordered forward. The Scots had not expected this charge and reeled back in disorder. Rokeby now fell on Douglas and the two Scottish wings were defeated. The King's division was outnumbered and the arrival of English reinforcements under Lord Lucy finished the battle. David II was captured trying to escape over the Browney bridge. The following year Percy led a raid into Scotland which met with little resistance.

Neville's Cross today:

The battle is not named after the English leader but after a more ancient cross, the stump of which remains near a roundabout on the Durham-Sunderland road. The ravine and country round the area are now much built up but the impression of height is apparent from the railway line which crosses the English position and looks down over the river, castle and cathedral.

OTTERBURN, 19th August, 1388
Northumberland O/S Landranger 80 (880 940)

During the minority of Richard II, the Scots, divided into two armies, crossed the border and the Earl of Douglas, with the smaller army, was beaten off when he had reached Newcastle by Harry Percy and his son Ralph who had an army of 7,000 mostly mounted, lightly armed soldiers. Douglas retreated with Percy's lance pennant and young Percy, determined to retrieve it, followed close behind.

Making for the border, the Scots attempted to capture Otterburn castle in Redesdale. This attempt failed so they camped in a wood nearby keeping a sharp lookout for Percy. The latter detected their camp at about midday on 19th August and, dividing his forces into two, set about the Scots

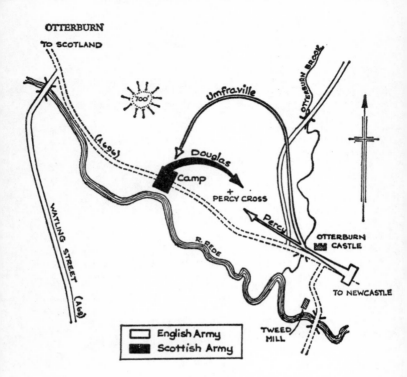

Battle of Otterburn, 1388

who were resting from their fruitless attacks on the castle. Sending Sir Thomas Umfraville on a wide detour to attack the Scots in the rear, Percy led his main body against their outposts on the slope before the camp. By this time it was dark and Douglas, with his main body, must have passed close to Umfraville without either party seeing the other. Making a flank attack the Scots fell upon the English and captured the two Percies. In the *mêleé* Douglas was killed but the Scots had other leaders present like the Earl of Dunbar, who led his men without his helmet, having had no time to prepare himself owing to the surprise of the English attack.

The battle was over by the following morning and Umfraville, who had attacked an empty camp and returned by the way he had come, led the English back to Newcastle, turning to capture several pursuers at one point, while Dunbar led the Scots back to Scotland. The Percies were not prisoners for long for in 1399 they joined Henry of Lancaster when he landed at Ravenspur to take the throne from the unfortunate Richard II.

Otterburn today:

The small village of Otterburn is famous for its army camp and its tweed mill. It is 32 miles north of Newcastle on the A696 to Scotland. The Percy Cross which marks the site of the battle is in a walled-off enclosure near the school on the right of the road going towards Scotland. It was erected by the local landowner at the request of the Earl of Northumberland in 1777 and is not a cross but a standing stone on a plinth. Nothing remains of the castle.

HOMILDON HILL, 14th September, 1402
Northumberland O/S Landranger 75 (969 295)

In summer 1402 King Henry IV took an army to Wales and during his absence a Scottish army of nearly 10,000 men under Archibald, Earl of Douglas, and Murdoch Stewart, son of the Duke of Albany, crossed the border laying waste to Northumberland as far as the Tyne.

The English commander in the north was Percy, Earl of Northumberland, and he raised an army with his son Hotspur and the refugee Earl of March, a Scot out of league with Douglas and Albany. Percy's army set out from Dunstanburgh to Wooler where they camped north of the village on the Till in a position that would block the passage of the Scots when they returned towards Coldstream and the border. Douglas reached Wooler before his scouts gave him warning of the English army so he drew up his ranks on the flat-topped Homildon Hill just outside Wooler. Percy had detached his 500 archers and positioned them on the opposite hill. By firing in ranks and withdrawing, the archers carefully led the Scots down to a field known as Red Riggs where the mounted English horsemen were ready for them. The Scots, angered by the English archers, probably outnumbered the English but their archers had short bows which did not have the range to reach the English ranks. Sir John Swinton, a border knight, and Adam Gordon, who for many years had been

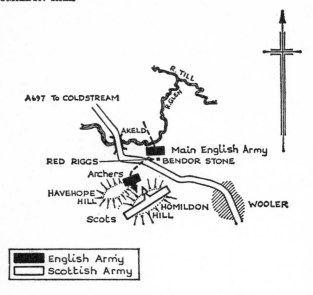

Battle of Homildon Hill, 1402

his rival, led a Scottish charge of 100 lances but it was cut down by the heavily armed English troops. Douglas himself was wounded and captured along with Murdoch Stewart and the earls of Moray, Angus and Orkney.

The retreating Scots were pursued as far as Coldstream where many were killed crossing the Tweed. The English longbow was the real winner of Homildon but the Scottish prisoners led to the downfall of Hotspur. He refused to give them up to the King and the wily Douglas persuaded him to attempt to join forces with Owen Glendower's Welsh army. The following year thus saw the eclipse of both Hotspur and Douglas at Shrewsbury (see below), the battle at which the young Prince Henry won his spurs.

Homildon Hill today:

The hill marked on the map as Humbleton Hill is two miles north-west of Wooler and in the field opposite is a battle stone. Red Riggs field is on the other side of the A697. The

32

1. *Ethandun, 878: the Westbury White Horse.*

2. *Stamford Bridge, 1066: the memorial stone on the green.*

3. Lewes, 1264: the gateway to Lewes Castle.

4. *Evesham, 1265: the memorial cross in All Saints churchyard.*

5. *Evesham, 1265: memorial stone to de Montfort erected in 1965.*

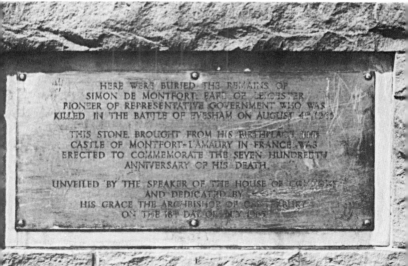

HERE WERE BURIED THE REMAINS OF
SIMON DE MONTFORT EARL OF LEICESTER
PIONEER OF REPRESENTATIVE GOVERNMENT WHO WAS
KILLED IN THE BATTLE OF EVESHAM ON AUGUST 4TH 1265

THIS STONE BROUGHT FROM HIS BIRTHPLACE THE
CASTLE OF MONTFORT-L'AMAURY IN FRANCE WAS
ERECTED TO COMMEMORATE THE SEVEN HUNDREDTH
ANNIVERSARY OF HIS DEATH.

UNVEILED BY THE SPEAKER OF THE HOUSE OF COMMONS
AND DEDICATED BY
HIS GRACE THE ARCHBISHOP OF CANTERBURY
ON THE 18TH DAY OF JULY 1965

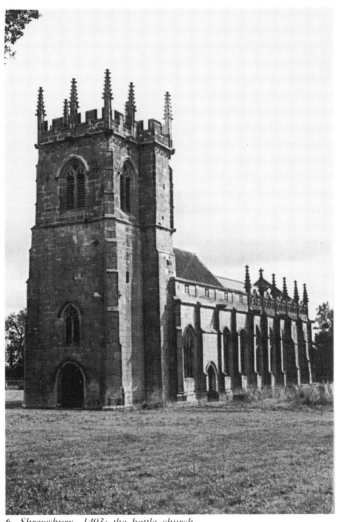

6. *Shrewsbury, 1403: the battle church.*

7. *Shrewsbury, 1403: one of the gargoyles on the battle church, supposed to depict the rebels.*

8. *St Albans, 1455: plaque to the Duke of Somerset on the site of the Castle Inn.*

ON THIS SITE STOOD
THE CASTLE INN
BEFORE WHICH
EDMUND BEAUFORT
2ND DUKE OF SOMERSET,
WAS SLAIN DURING
THE 1ST BATTLE OF ST ALBANS
22ND. MAY 1455.

9. *Blore Heath, 1459: the memorial cross.*

10. *Blore Heath, 1459: the inscription on the cross.*

ON THIS SPOT
WAS FOUGHT THE BATTLE
OF BLORE HEATH 1459.
LORD AUDLEY
WHO COMMANDED FOR
THE SIDE OF LANCASTER
WAS DEFEATED AND SLAIN.
THIS MONUMENT WAS
RESTORED BY THE TYRLEY
PARISH COUNCIL TO MARK
THE 500TH ANNIVERSARY
OF THE BATTLE

11. *Northampton, 1460: Delapré Abbey.*

12. *Wakefield, 1460: Sandal Castle.*

This Memorial is erected to perpetuate the Memory of an obstinate, bloody, and decisive battle fought near this Spot in the civil Wars between the ambitious Houses of York and Lancaster, on the 2ᵈ Day of February 1461, between the Forces of *Edward Mortimer* Earl of March, (afterwards *Edward the Fourth*) on the Side of York and those of *Henry the Sixth*, on the Side of Lancaster.

The King's Troops were commanded by *Jasper* Earl of Pembroke, *Edward* commanded his own in Person and was victorious. The Slaughter was great on both Sides Four Thousand being left dead on the Field and many Welsh Persons of the first distinction were taken Prisoners among whom was *Owen Tudor* (Great-Grandfather to *Henry* the *Eighth* and a Descendent of the illustrious *Cadwallader*) who was afterwards beheaded at Hereford

This was the decisive battle which fixed *Edward* the *Fourth* on the Throne of England who was proclaimed King in London on the Fifth of March following.

Erected by Subscription Year 1799

13. *Mortimer's Cross, 1461: the monument to the battle.*

40

English archers were probably on Havehope Hill and descended to the river near Akeld where they joined the main English force that had crossed the river. There is another battle stone between Yeavering and Old Yeavering, but as bones have been dug up at Red Riggs it is assumed that this is where the main action took place.

SHREWSBURY, 21st July, 1403

Shropshire O/S Landranger 126 (515 170)

Henry IV came to the throne in 1399 having deposed Richard II with the help of the Percies. The start of his reign was a continuous struggle against rebellions. The Scots were defeated by the Percies at Homildon Hill in 1402 but Owen Glendower remained undefeated in Wales where he was joined by Edmund Mortimer. Northumberland, the elder Percy, and his son Harry Hotspur pressed for money to carry on the war against Glendower. In 1403 King Henry demanded that they submit their Scottish prisoner, the Earl of Douglas. But the Percies rebelled, proclaiming that Richard II had been starved to death by Henry and that the Earl of March, Mortimer's nephew, was the rightful heir to the throne. Douglas and Glendower planned to join them and Hotspur moved south from Chester to join up with the Welsh.

The King's young son Henry, Shakespeare's famous Prince Hal, was at Shrewsbury with a small army. The King moved from Lichfield to Stafford and joined his son on 20th July, arriving in time to cut off Hotspur from Glendower. Camping for the night at Berwick on the Severn, he discovered that he was in danger of being cut off from Chester by the advancing enemy, so he positioned his army on a slope, now known as Battlefield, some three miles north of Shrewsbury. Prince Hal's men were on the left and the King with the main force was on the right. The royal army numbered about 12,000, some 2,000 more than Hotspur's force. Both armies were using the longbow and the Cheshire bowmen soon halted the King's advance. Hotspur attacked on the left wing and centre. Douglas and Hotspur with a small handful of men tried to reach and cut down the King, but before they got far, Prince Hal, whose men were getting the better of their opponents, suddenly turned to the right and attacked

41

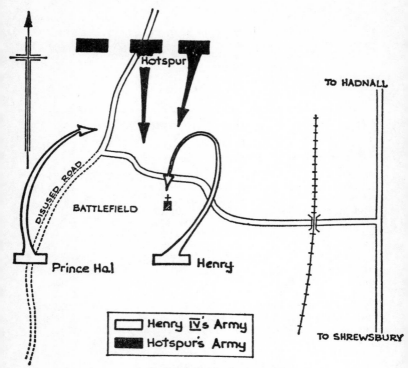

Battle of Shrewsbury, 1403

Hotspur in the rear. Young Hal was wounded but refused to leave the field and Hotspur was killed by an arrow. The rebels fled and thus ended "the worst battle that ever came to England and the unkindest"

Shrewsbury today:

Take the A49 out of Shrewsbury towards Whitchurch and after the Market Drayton turning to the right, take the first left down a narrow dead-end that goes under the railway. The church is in the middle of the battlefield. The surrounding terrain is mostly flat but there is a slight ridge at right angles to

42

the railway on the other side of the road to the church and this marks Hotspur's position. The church was founded by Henry IV as a chantry chapel to a nearby college in memory of the fallen. Inside are the crests of the victors. Some of the gargoyles are supposed to represent the rebels.

ST. ALBANS, 22nd May, 1455
Hertfordshire O/S Landranger 166 (149 072)

The Wars of the Roses, which started with the Battle of St. Albans in 1455, were a series of disjointed wars between the rival families in power at Court. The European Hundred Years' War had come to an end and England was full of ex-servicemen who were kept in the pay of the large landowners. The archers, pikemen and knights never really put down their arms, but it was a private quarrel and the ordinary country tradesmen went about their work undisturbed by national events. King Henry VI, deeply religious, was not powerful enough to keep order, but in 1455 he shook off a fit of insanity and reinstated Somerset as his Chief Councillor, sending his disgruntled cousin, Richard, Duke of York, to Yorkshire. Many considered that York's right to the throne was as good as Henry's and, aided by the powerful Earl of Warwick, Richard marched his army of 3,000 veterans of the French wars south towards St. Albans.

Somerset and Henry collected a force of about 2,000 and moved out of London to Watford and St. Albans which they reached just before Richard. Barricades were thrown up in Sopwell Street and Victoria Street, the Royal standard being in St. Peter's Street (opposite Woolworths!). The first Yorkist attack was held up at these barricades by Lords Clifford and Somerset. Warwick led his troops between the two streets along the line of the present London road and finding no resistance, turned left and right to attack the rear of the barricades. Somerset was killed outside the Castle Inn (now the National Westminster Bank, where a plaque commemorates the event), Clifford died bravely at a barricade; Stafford, son of the Duke of Buckingham who had tried to make peace before the battle, and the Duke of Northumberland were also killed. The Yorkist victory was complete but the captured Henry was still treated as king and the victorious Yorkists went down on bended knees to kiss his hand. The governing Council was reorganised and there was peace for about four years but Henry's queen, Margaret, who had taken sanctuary

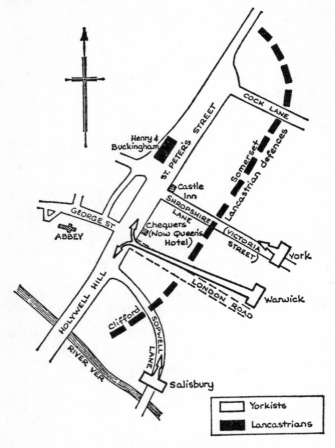

Battle of St. Albans, 1455

with her son in St. Albans Abbey, was determined to raise the Lancastrian standard once more. Before bloodshed broke out again there was an attack from an unexpected quarter. The French raided Sandwich in Kent and Warwick was despatched to sea to defend the realm. There was a brief reconciliation

44

and the sons of the defeated Lancastrians walked hand-in-hand in procession with the Yorkists to St. Paul's, led by York and the Queen. It was only a token gesture, but for a moment the Queen's French blood was forgotten and her party grew in strength.

In 1461 another battle was fought at St. Albans in which Queen Margaret got her revenge. It was a larger and very different affair and Warwick, who had been the victor of the first battle, was lucky to escape with his life.

St. Albans today:

One of the oldest towns in England, St. Albans has not changed its main streets in shape or direction since 1455 with the exception of the London Road, which is new and follows the line of Warwick's advance.

BLORE HEATH, 23rd September, 1459
Staffordshire O/S Landranger 127 (713 352)

The first Battle of St. Albans in 1455 ended with an uneasy four-year truce. By 1459 the Duke of York was apprehensive about the Queen's behaviour. She monopolised the King's Council with her favourite, the Earl of Wiltshire, and in Cheshire she was distributing the badge of the swan—the sign of the Prince of Wales, her son—to men who joined the Lancastrian army. The Duke set out for Wales to raise an army and Lord Salisbury, father of Warwick the Kingmaker who was in Calais, went to Middleham in Yorkshire to equip his faithful Yorkists and then set out for Ludlow with 5,000 men.

The plan was to unite the two Yorkist armies at Ludlow castle and march on London. Queen Margaret was well informed. She and Henry were in Nottingham in September but moved to Eccleshall with the large Lancastrian army. She detached Lord Audley with nearly 10,000 men to arrest Salisbury and he blocked Salisbury's way outside Market Drayton. The wily Salisbury suspected the move or, more probably, his spies told him the position of the Lancastrians, for he moved off the Newcastle-under-Lyme road and took up a position overlooking Hemphill Brook. He carefully con-

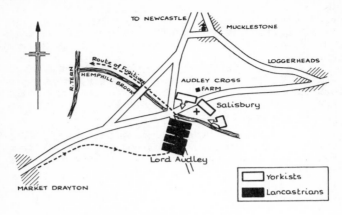

Battle of Blore Heath, 1459

cealed his two wings behind the slope so that Lord Audley, advancing, saw only the central body and promptly attacked on a narrow front. Salisbury made a feint retreat and then brought up his wings when the heavily mounted knights were crossing the steep-sided brook. Twice the Lancastrians tried to charge and the spears and bills of the Yorkists beat them back. At the second charge Lord Audley was killed. Much earlier 500 Lancashire men had defected from his army. The third charge was unmounted and the Cheshire archers were hemmed in too much to use their bows and so were easy targets for the Yorkist archers. Many fled along the stream bed to where it joins the river Tern and were killed in the stampede to get across.

The 2,000 Lancastrian dead included Sir Thomas Dutton, Sir Hugh Venables and Sir John Leigh. Salisbury had won one of the most overwhelming victories in the Wars of the Roses but it only led to the defeat of the Yorkists, when their forces did meet at Ludlow, at Ludford Bridge, when the powerful Calais garrison deserted to the Queen's army under their able leader Sir Andrew Trollope. Lord Salisbury had to flee to France with the other Yorkists.

Blore Heath today:

The battlefield lies across the main A53 Market Drayton to Newcastle-under-Lyme road. To find the cross, which is in the field opposite Audley Cross farm, it is best to stop by the crossroads about four miles from Market Drayton. Park in one of the side roads. The cross is in the field on the other side of the brook and can only just be seen from the A53 when there are no crops. The road to the left goes to the village of Mucklestone where there is a plaque on a cottage facing an inscribed anvil in the churchyard denoting that Queen Margaret, having seen from the church tower that her army had lost, made off with the shoes on her horse hastily reversed by Shufnall the local smith, whose descendants have a gravestone in the churchyard. How she found herself 'behind enemy lines' is not clear and the legend is improbable.

NORTHAMPTON, 10th July, 1460

Northamptonshire O/S Landranger 152 (759 957)

In October 1459 the Yorkists were defeated at Ludford Bridge and a Lancastrian army captured Ludlow Castle. Warwick, Edward the Earl of March (later Edward IV), and other Yorkists fled to Calais, York himself going to Ireland. After raiding Sandwich and capturing Lord Rivers, Warwick landed at Sandwich with a small force strengthened by the addition of soldiers from the Calais garrison. London opened its gates to the Yorkist army but part of Warwick's force had to be left behind under Lord Salisbury to lay siege to the Tower, which was held by the Lancastrians.

Henry, Margaret and the Duke of Buckingham were in Coventry collecting an army. From here they moved to Northampton where just south-east of the city they entrenched themselves in a bend of the river Nene facing south away from the river. "High banks and deep trenches" were thrown up, as Hall's Chronicle relates; the King "studies nothing but of peace, quiet and solitary life," so it was left to Margaret and Buckingham to prepare for the battle. Lord Grey of Ruthin, a cousin of the Queen, defended the right flank, Buckingham the left and the archers were in the centre. March and Warwick spent the night of 9th July on Hunsbury Hill, where there are still traces of a hill fort. Before it was light they attacked—Edward's men leading—across the Nene marshes

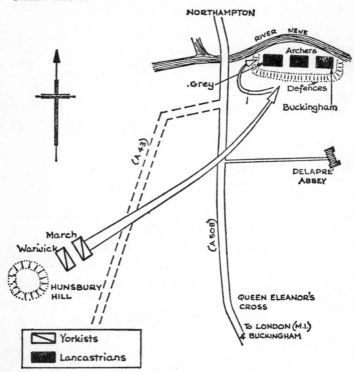

Battle of Northampton, 1460

by Delapré Abbey. Watching on nearby Queen Eleanor's Cross were the Archbishop of Canterbury and the Papal Legate, who had tried to arbitrate the day before without success.

It was pouring with rain all day and Edward's mounted infantry were stuck in the mud, where they were easy prey for the King's archers. The defending cannon were drenched but pointed wooden spikes kept out the horsemen. Buckingham had nearly won the day, but suddenly the unexpected happened.

Lord Grey, perhaps influenced by the fact that the Archbishop and the Papal Legate had arrived with Warwick, suddenly ordered his men to lay down their arms. The Yorkists poured over the defences and attacked Buckingham's flank. Behind, the swollen river Nene took its toll of the desperate fleeing Royal army. Buckingham, Shrewsbury, Lord Beaumont and Lord Egremont were among the slain. The king was taken to London and lodged at the Bishop's palace and York came over from Ireland to claim the throne. Queen Margaret and a few Lancastrians escaped to Chester, while in London the lords agreed to make York Protector and heir apparent during Henry's lifetime.

Northampton today:

Enter the city by A508 from the M1 junction and before the railway on the right is a large park. At the end of this is Delapré Abbey, now mostly 16th and 19th century. It is open to the public on Saturday and Thursday afternoons all the year round and contains the Northamptonshire Record Office. The Eleanor Cross stands outside the grounds on the main road. The actual battle was fought by the river and the nearest you can get to the site is in Nunn Mills Road by the Avon Cosmetics factory. The Delapré Abbey stable cupola is just visible from here but the Archbishop and the Legate must have had very keen eyesight to see the battle from the cross in the middle of a storm.

WAKEFIELD, 31st December, 1460

Yorkshire O/S Landranger 110 (337 183)

The Battle of Northampton installed the Duke of York as Protector for the third time but when the Duke actually claimed the throne for himself, many thronged to Queen Margaret's banner. York, advised by Lord Salisbury, set off with an army of 5,000 for the north. The Earl of March went to the Welsh border to raise reinforcements and Warwick remained in London. It was a fatal decision—the Lancastrians were united at Hull, the Yorkists were divided.

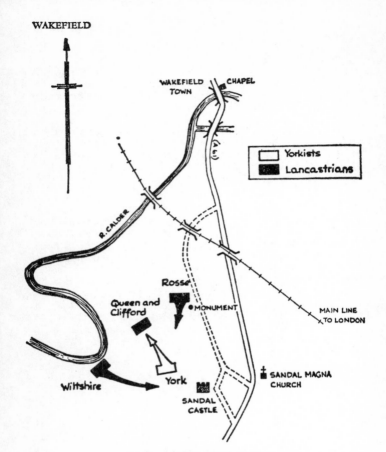

WAKEFIELD

WAKEFIELD TOWN

CHAPEL

☐ Yorkists
■ Lancastrians

R. CALDER

Rosse

Queen and
Clifford

● MONUMENT

MAIN LINE
TO LONDON

Wiltshire

York

SANDAL
CASTLE

✝ SANDAL MAGNA
CHURCH

Battle of Wakefield, 1460

After a skirmish at Worksop, York arrived at Sandal castle and decided to remain there until his reinforcements arrived. Margaret, with an army of 18,000, approached from York and cunningly posted a detachment of her troops on Sandal common in full view of the castle. The main body of the Lancastrian army under Lord Clifford was divided into two groups—the foot under the Earl of Wiltshire and the horse under Lord Roos. Clifford placed them out of sight of the castle.

The ruse worked. York, perhaps faced by the possible choice of death by starvation or battle, chose the latter. He may have been taunted by the Queen into action but he was naturally impatient and against the advice of Sir David Hall and old Salisbury, he decided to attack the Queen's army. The impact of the Yorkist charge broke the Lancastrian line and a great struggle took place. Clifford did not pause. Sending Roos and Wiltshire into the attack he caught York "like unto fish in a net". Wiltshire captured Sandal castle which was undefended and Clifford caught the unfortunate Earl of Rutland, York's eighteen-year-old son, on Wakefield bridge where he killed him outright having sworn to avenge his father's death at York's hand at St. Albans in 1455.

The Duke was also killed along with 2,900 Yorkists. Old Salisbury was taken to Pontefract castle where he was imprisoned only to be dragged out by the Lancastrian mob and murdered. The heads of the Yorkist leaders were stuck on the Micklegate Bar in York so "York might overlook York". Lord Clifford had his revenge but there were two Yorkists left to continue the struggle—Edward, later Edward IV and his brother Richard, later Richard III.

Wakefield today:

The A61 leads out of Wakefield towards Barnsley and Sandal Magna is the first suburb it reaches. The remains of the castle are at the end of Castle Road. The battle was fought on the field near the entrance. The monument to the Duke of York was knocked down by the Roundheads after Sandal surrendered in 1645 but in 1897 the present memorial was erected in the grounds of Manygates School and contains a carving of the Duke based on the statue of him that used to stand on the Welsh bridge at Shrewsbury. The chapel on Wakefield bridge, supposed to have been endowed by Edward IV in memory of the Earl of Rutland, was built in the fourteenth century.

MORTIMER'S CROSS, 2nd February, 1461
Herefordshire O/S 129 Landranger 149 (427 637)

The loss of his father and elder brother at Wakefield in January 1460 must have been a terrible shock for young Edward, Earl of March. He was at Shrewsbury over Christmas and travelled to Gloucester where he heard the dreadful news. Jasper Tudor, Earl of Pembroke, and the Earl of Ormonde, with their army of French, Irish and Welsh, many of whom had crossed to Wales from France, were determined to capture him. The Earl of Warwick was in London preparing to lead the Yorkists north against Queen Margaret so young Edward had to rely on his faithful 'Marchers', mostly farmers from the Welsh border, many of whom were well mounted but poorly armed.

The Lancastrians were marching east towards Worcester to try to get between Edward and Warwick. Moving north through Hereford, Edward, who must have been well served by scouts, placed his small army in Wig Marsh north of Leominster overlooking the Lugg river and the road junction now known as Mortimer's Cross. In the early morning of 2nd February his men were startled by the strange sight of three suns in the sky. Taking this as a religious omen representing the Trinity, the Yorkists knelt in prayer. They rose to find that the three suns were now one and that the vanguard of the Lancastrians was approaching.

The battle started at daybreak and continued until dusk. Edward held his ground. Sir Richard Croft who lived at nearby Croft Castle knew the lie of the land well and advised Edward to let the enemy attack. Pembroke put Ormonde's vanguard against Edward's right wing and sent the main body of his troops against Edward's centre. Ormonde's men chased Edward's off the field but by the time they returned to help Pembroke, the latter had been defeated. Three thousand men lay dead. The grandfather of Henry VII, Owen Tudor, was captured by the local Leominster men in the village of Kingsland. His son, Jasper, escaped with the Earl of Ormonde towards Hereford. Owen Tudor was executed in Hereford market place. "That head shall lie on the stock that was wont to lie on Queen Katherine's lap," he said as he mounted the scaffold. He was the second husband of the mother of Henry VI—so he was a notable Lancastrian loss.

Just over two weeks later the Earl of Warwick was

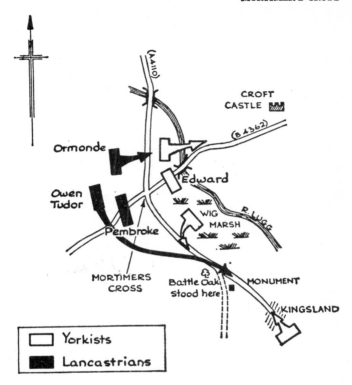

Battle of Mortimer's Cross, 1461

beaten at St. Albans by the Queen and the King was rescued. Edward, hurrying east to help, met the luckless Warwick and his survivors at Chipping Norton in Oxfordshire. Owen Tudor's death had delayed Edward sufficiently from riding to help Warwick. Margaret was in command but the stage was set for the largest battle of the Wars of the Roses—Towton.

Mortimer's Cross today:

The monument erected in 1799 is at the junction of A4110 from Hereford and B4360 from Leominster. The public house is also called The Monument. There is no sign

53

today of the Battle Oak that stood nearby. At the cross-roads a mile and a half to the north is a hotel and a garage. Edward would have occupied the east bank of the Lugg and his scouts at Mortimer's Rock on the Shobdon road could have signalled to him on Pembroke's approach. Nearby Croft Castle is open to the public and Sir Richard Croft's memorial is in the church. He died in 1507 and was a veteran of the battles of Stoke and Tewkesbury as well as Mortimer's Cross.

TOWTON, 29th March, 1461

Yorkshire O/S Landranger 105 (479 379)

In 1461 the second battle of St. Albans resulted in a Lancastrian victory and the townspeople of London, Yorkists for the most part, were so alarmed that trade stopped and men buried their valuables. For nine days Margaret did nothing and the young Yorkist, Edward, returning from his victory at Mortimer's Cross, arrived in London with the Earl of Warwick and the remnants of the defeated army from St. Albans.

The Yorkists were quick to reorganise their army. Lord Fauconberg raised the Kentish Yorkists, the Earl of Warwick brought in supporters from the Midlands and Edward himself made for Pontefract where the Yorkist army joined together to face the Lancastrians who were positioned at Towton, ten miles south of York. Edward had declared himself King Edward IV at Westminster before he left London.

The Lancastrians, numbering (according to Hall's *Chronicle*) over 30,000, were positioned north of the Aire river and on 28th March the Earl of Warwick and Lord Fitzwalter tried to hold part of the north bank near Ferrybridge against an overwhelming Lancastrian attack led by Lord Clifford. Fitzwalter was killed and Warwick extricated his men with difficulty. Lord Fauconberg with the Yorkist van then crossed the river upstream at Castleford and caught Clifford's retiring force in the flank. Clifford was killed by an arrow and the entire Yorkist army, in numbers slightly less than the Lancastrians, but as yet without the Duke of Norfolk's men who were on their way from East Anglia, crossed the river and formed a line on a ridge north of Saxton facing the enemy. Across a slight dip the Lancastrians stood on a similar ridge.

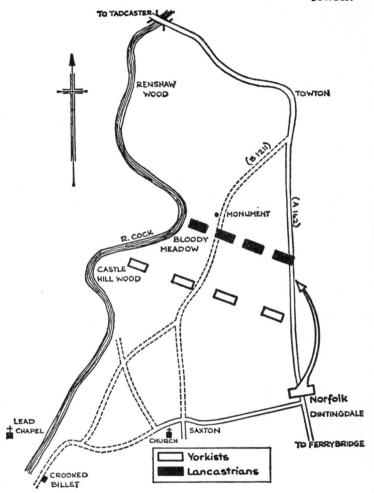

Battle of Towton, 1461

Henry VI did not want to fight on Palm Sunday, but his captains, Northumberland, Somerset and Lord Dacre took command. The Yorkist Fauconberg, a small wily experienced soldier, ordered his archers to fire and step back. The strong wind and driving snow were blowing hard at the Lancastrian ranks, so their archers when returning the fire found that their arrows fell short.

The Lancastrians now advanced and the Earl of Warwick suddenly found he was bearing the brunt of the attack. The Yorkists held on grimly. Large numbers of dead and wounded confused and interfered with the battle. On the west flank a group of Lancastrians surprised the Yorkists in Castle Hill Wood and Edward's line began to bend. Two hours after the initial clash of arms Norfolk's men arrived to aid the Yorkists and proceeded to advance on the right wing towards Towton. The Lancastrian left wing was soon out-flanked and they began to retreat towards the bridge over the river Cock on the Towton-Tadcaster road. The river banks are very steep here and it is probable the Cock was in flood The slaughter at the bridge was very great and also at Tadcaster where there was an attempted stand by a few Lancastrians.

The casualties in this, the largest battle of the Wars of the Roses, were enormous. King Edward reckoned there were 28,000, but this is no doubt an exaggeration. Certainly the Lancastrians lost the flower of their chivalry. The Earls of Devonshire and Wiltshire were beheaded after the battle; Lord Dacre was shot in the head by a bolt from a crossbow while resting with his helmet off during a lull in the battle; Henry VI was ultimately captured and imprisoned in the Tower; the Queen and her son fled to France. The Battle of Towton ensured the rule of Edward IV but did not end the Wars of the Roses.

Towton today:

Take the A64 out of York and turn on to the A162 at Tadcaster. The first hamlet you come to is Towton. Turn right here to Saxton. Lord Dacre's cross is on the hill on the right and dates from the late fifteenth century. In Saxton churchyard is his grave, rather dilapidated but recognisable for its coat-of-arms showing a quartered chequered shield. In a field opposite the 'Crooked Billet' near the little Cock river is the small Lead chapel, which although much older than the fifteenth century, appears surprisingly to have no gravestones from the battle. Further up the hill is a farm track which has to one side of it two grave mounds, now barely recognisable as such.

EDGECOTE, 26th July, 1469

Northamptonshire O/S Landranger 151 (519 468)

The battles of Northampton and Towton put Edward IV on the throne but he depended on his friends the Earl of Warwick and the Nevilles to maintain the peace of England, and in those troubled years of the Wars of the Roses there was little peace for the nobility. In 1464 Edward married Elizabeth Woodville, the widow of a Lancastrian knight and daughter of the Duke of Bedford's steward. This rash step was followed by the rise of the Woodville family in court and government. When Edward married his sister to Charles of Burgundy, thus jeopardising England's relationship with France, it was too much for Warwick; he went to Calais

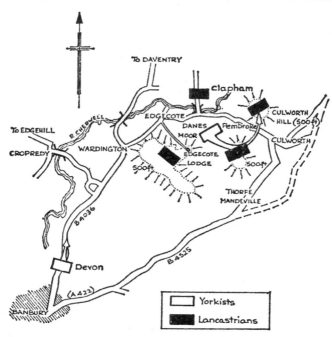

Battle of Edgecote, 1469

with Clarence and waited there, prepared to return and oppose Edward when the time was right.

In the north a new figure suddenly appeared on the scene —Robin of Redesdale. Protesting against the 'thrave' tax, Robin (who was a Yorkshire knight, Sir John Conyers) raised an army of bowmen under the Warwick banner of the ragged staff. When Clarence and Warwick landed at Sandwich in May, Robin had already moved south and Edward, with a very small army, went to Nottingham. Proclaiming that his daughter Isabel was to marry Clarence, Warwick now ordered Robin's troops to cut Edward off from London. Edward, realising his danger, summoned William Herbert, Lord Pembroke, and his brother from Wales, where they had recently captured Harlech castle. A more formidable army of bowmen under Humphry Stafford, newly created Lord Devon, joined Pembroke and made for Northampton where they hoped to prevent Robin's army at Leicester from linking up with Warwick's men, who had reached London in July.

On 25th July Devon and Pembroke quarrelled at Banbury about their billets and Devon led his men away to Deddington, where they were protected in the castle, while Pembroke took the Daventry road and camped at Edgecote, seven miles north of Banbury near Wardington. On 26th July Pembroke, who was an experienced but somewhat foolhardy soldier, saw the rebel army occupying three hills around his position. His way out of this would have been to withdraw to join Devon. Instead he attacked. With remarkable dash his Welshmen captured the centre hill and, turning left, attacked Culworth Hill. Young Richard Herbert twice passed through "the battail of his adversaries without any mortal wound", killing many with his poleaxe. Robin's men received fresh supplies of arrows and those on Culworth Hill forced Pembroke back on to Danes Moor. Here he was out of bowshot range and his Welsh spearmen began to force back the advancing rebels. Warwick had meanwhile sent off a small advance force under John Clapham of Skipton, a veteran of Towton. Joined by some Northampton roughs, Clapham suddenly appeared in Pembroke's rear with shouts of "A Warwick, A Warwick" and the battle was over. Both Herberts were executed at Northampton. Lord Devon, who had arrived when it was all over, escaped to Somerset, where he was killed by an angry street mob. Robin's young son was killed together with 168 knights, squires and gentlemen of both sides. Edward with his brother Richard had taken refuge at Olney. Here Warwick's brother, the Archbishop of York, captured them and the Nevilles were supreme until defeated at Barnet in 1471.

Edgecote today:

This is a beautiful part of Northamptonshire, strangely forgotten, and the battlefield can be clearly seen by taking the B4036 out of Banbury to Wardington, turning right and driving round Danes Moor through Thorpe Mandeville and Culworth. Edgecote Lodge stands high on the hill overlooking Pembroke's position.

The road across the Cherwell and up to Aston le Walls is known as Welsh Road; it was the only escape route for the Welsh spearmen and Hays Bridge, where Clapham appeared, is well concealed from Danes Moor. Edgecote House and church make an attractive group and the thirteenth-century church is full of monuments to the Chauncey family, but they do not appear to have figured in the battle.

BARNET, 14th April, 1471

Hertfordshire O/S Landranger 166 (248 977)

The Yorkists came to power in 1461 after their victory at the Battle of Towton. Edward IV, whose father the Duke of York had been killed a few months earlier at Wakefield, was crowned at Westminster. The Lancastrian cause was by no means dead and Edward struggled to keep the country in order. The Earl of Warwick, no friend of the Woodvilles—Edward had married Elizabeth Woodville—plotted with Queen Margaret to put Henry VI back on the throne. Supported by Clarence, Edward's brother, and the Marquis of Montagu, Edward found his army outnumbered at Doncaster. On 30th September, accompanied by Richard, Hastings and Earl Rivers, he escaped to Burgundy from King's Lynn. Henry was king once more and many Yorkists fled for their lives. Duke Charles of Burgundy lent men and money to Edward to reclaim his crown, and the Yorkist army set sail on 11th March 1471.

On 14th March Edward of York landed at Ravenspur with a force of French and Flemish troops. Between him and London, where his wife and Yorkist spies were hastily gathering recruits, was the Earl of Warwick, his former friend, now a bitter enemy. Warwick's army was at Coventry but the Earl was anxious to gain reinforcements before he attacked. At the gates of Coventry Clarence intervened joining his brother with several thousand men and the Yorkists marched south and entered London in triumph. Warwick, Exeter and Montagu followed at a distance and set up their positions near

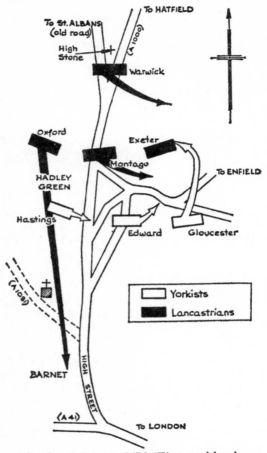

Battle of Barnet, 1471 (First positions)

Barnet on 13th April, blocking Edward's route to the north.
Time was on Warwick's side for Queen Margaret was on
her way to help him. With Montagu blocking the St. Albans
road, the Earl of Oxford on the right and the Earl of Exeter
on the left Warwick held a strong position and he placed himself at the rear with the guns and reserve. His army was about

60

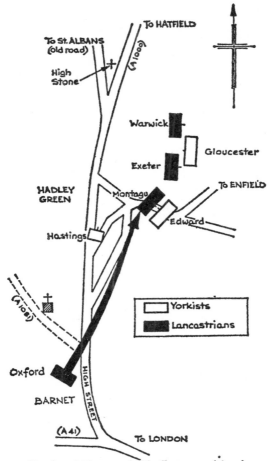

Battle of Barnet, 1471 (Later positions)

15,000 compared with the Yorkists' 10,000. Edward arrived and positioned his troops at night, so he was not able to see Warwick's position. Richard, Duke of Gloucester, on the right wing thus outflanked Exeter. Oxford outflanked Lord Hastings on Edward's left.

Easter Day, 1471, was very foggy as this part of

Hertfordshire can be. Visibility was down to about twenty yards. Both armies advanced and only Edward and Montagu found each other at first. Neither gave ground and on the right flank Richard found he had to turn left to find Exeter's flank where his sudden attack caused both Exeter and Warwick to turn about and face him. Oxford, the most efficient soldier on either side, apart from Edward himself, attacked Hastings's flank and pursued some of his men to Barnet and beyond. Meanwhile, Montagu had turned his men to keep in line with Exeter, so that when Oxford rallied his men and returned to the fight his expected charge on Edward caught the rear of Montagu's troops instead. It was with cries of "Treason, Treason" that Montagu's archers turned and fired at Oxford.

The battle was over. Montagu was killed and his brother Warwick attempting to walk to his horse in Wrotham wood was overtaken by men less heavily armed, knocked down and slaughtered. Oxford escaped north to fight again at another more successful battle—Bosworth Field. Edward IV was king and the unfortunate Henry VI, who was more interested in books than battles, had neither power nor desire to prevent it.

Barnet today:

Take the A1 out of London and turn right on the A411 to Barnet. Carry on for about a mile down the High Street to Hadley Green. At a road junction is a tall monument erected in 1740 which has been used at one time as a signpost. The simple inscription says that 'Here was fought the famous battle of Barnet'. To your left is the golf course where the Earl of Oxford attacked, to your right is Hadley Common where Richard held his ground. In spite of the houses everywhere, there is a remarkable amount of common land here still and it is not difficult to imagine the Earl's troops returning from Barnet village to attack the rear of the Marquis of Montagu's men.

TEWKESBURY, 4th May, 1471

Gloucestershire O/S Landranger 150 (890 318)

On the same day as the Battle of Barnet, Henry's Queen and her son with a small but desperate band of Lancastrians landed at Weymouth. Edward IV heard the news two days later and promptly organised his army at Windsor. Although short of arms and equipment, Margaret found both at Bristol where she was warmly welcomed, but few men joined her

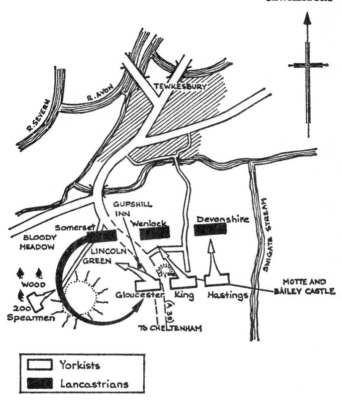

Battle of Tewkesbury, 1471

ranks. North of Bristol, Margaret discovered Edward would prevent her reaching Wales. She sent her vanguard to Sodbury Hill, where they created enough disturbance to convince Edward that he should spend the night there and prepare for battle in the morning. The following morning a scout gave Edward the news. Margaret was making for Gloucester after spending the night at Berkeley Castle. It was now a race for the river and Edward's scouts won. The gates of Gloucester were closed and the Queen's tired soldiers struggled on to arrive at Tewkesbury on 3rd May.

Lord Pembroke was hastily gathering a Lancastrian force in Wales but before it could appear Tewkesbury was fought. Near Gupshill Manor, Margaret placed her centre under Wenlock, a soldier who had fought for the Yorkists at Towton and was unreliable. The right wing was commanded by Somerset and the left by Devonshire. Her force was slightly larger than Edward's army which was arranged in three groups commanded by Gloucester, Edward himself and Lord Hastings.

On 4th May the two armies were about four hundred yards apart but between them on the ground was a mass of "evil land and deep dykes". Horsemen would be in trouble. Somerset, who had reconnoitred the ground, worked out a bold plan. He led his troops concealed behind a small hillock and descended on Richard of Gloucester's rear. It was a brilliant move but Edward had positioned 200 spearmen in the woods by the hillock and as soon as Somerset passed they attacked his rear, causing so much confusion that Somerset's men were surrounded and defeated.

In the centre Lord Wenlock, accompanied by Margaret's son, was keeping his ground when he suddenly found an angry Somerset beside him accusing him of cowardice and treachery for failing to support the right wing. Before Wenlock could reply Somerset knocked him dead with his mace. The centre now collapsed and the Lancastrians fled for the river and the sanctuary of Tewkesbury Abbey. Young Prince Edward was overtaken by Clarence, Edward IV's brother, and was killed before he could reach the abbey. Somerset was executed the following day with all the Lancastrian leaders and in London "the melancholy spectator" who had survived for so long, King Henry VI, was murdered in the Tower. The way to power was open at last for young Richard of Gloucester.

Tewkesbury today:

Tewkesbury now has a battle trail which can be joined from the car park off Church Street, close to the Abbey. It takes about 45 minutes to walk and is marked by metal posts. There is a plan at Bloody Meadow, one in the bar of Gupshill Manor Inn and another in Tewkesbury Museum. Gupshill Manor is on the A38 to Gloucester. It is difficult to accept that this building dates from over 40 years before the battle. On the other side of the A38 is Margaret's camp and the earthworks of a motte and bailey castle.

BOSWORTH FIELD, 22nd August, 1485

Leicestershire O/S Landranger 140 (405 005)

On Sunday 7th August 1485, Henry Tudor, Earl of Richmond, landed with 2,500 men at Milford Haven, after avoiding a hostile fleet under Viscount Lovell. He had promises of support but Richard III had an army four times larger and at this stage in the Wars of the Roses men like John Paston, who had been at Barnet, preferred to stay at home. The Welsh leader, Rhys ap Thomas, brought valuable support and Henry's small army now marched under the banner of the Dragon of Cadwallader. At Shrewsbury more soldiers joined them but Lord Stanley who had brought his Shropshire men to St. Alban's in 1455 to fight for Richard's father, made no promise of support. His son Lord Strange was held by Richard as a hostage and when the boy tried to escape at Nottingham, Richard found out the truth. Both Lord Stanley and his brother Sir William were for Henry, but fearing for Strange's life they did not dare commit their men to either side.

In East Anglia the Duke of Norfolk raised about 3,000 infantry; Northumberland came to Leicester with about the same number. Richard's army now reached 10,000 and in three columns it moved on to a strong position at Ambien Hill near Market Bosworth, blocking the road from Atherstone where Henry's 5,000 men were camping. Nearby Sir William Stanley's 2,500 mounted infantry and his brother's 3,500 foot soldiers waited for the battle to begin, neither Henry nor Richard sure which side they would take.

The Earl of Oxford, who supported Henry, had learnt to keep his men close to their standards after his disaster at Barnet. When Norfolk's force moved down Ambien Hill he formed a wedge formation, one flank protected by a marsh, the other flank open. Another 1,000 men joined Norfolk from the reserve and Oxford's hard fighting soldiers were slowly forced back by overwhelming numbers.

Bosworth Field

Richard had learnt from the battle of Tewkesbury that it was dangerous to hold a position on a hill, because although you can see the enemy you cannot always get to grips with them before they are surrounding you. He was anxious about the

Stanleys, because Sir William Stanley and his horsemen had now joined forces with Lord Stanley's horsemen and had positioned themselves between Sutton Cheney and Shenton so that they could still join either side. With Norfolk pressing hard on Richmond's vanguard under Oxford, Richard was anxious to get into the fray. He was upset that Northumberland refused to move and, seeing Richmond with his standard bearers riding out towards the Stanley camp, he determined to seize the initiative. Giving the order he charged down the hill to cut off Henry before the latter reached the Stanleys. It was a bold move and some hundreds of knights followed him, but they were not enough. Richard cut down Sir John Cheney with his axe and impaled William Brandon on his lance. Sir William Stanley did not hesitate but led his men quickly into the battle on Henry's side. Richard was unhorsed and cut down by Stanley's men. Only Northumberland could save him, for Norfolk had been killed by Oxford's men. However the battle was soon over and Northumberland fled without joining the battle. (In 1748 a pile of weapons were found near Sutton Cheney, believed to have been thrown there by the fleeing Yorkists.) Richard's body was stripped and taken to Leicester and Henry was crowned on the field.

Two years later there was Lambert Simnel's rising, quickly put down by Henry's yeoman army at Stoke near Newark. Viscount Lovell, who had escaped from Bosworth, in spite of taking part in Richard's charge, also escaped from Stoke by swimming the Trent with his horse. He lived in hiding in his ancient manor at Minster Lovell in the Oxfordshire Cotswolds, which, although a ruin, still has a tradition that a skeleton found in a sealed-off vault was the body of Richard's faithful admiral.

Bosworth today:

If you take the A5 from London, turn right about half a mile before Atherstone along an old Roman road to Sutton Cheney. In the church is a brass plate to Richard III put up in July 1967 by the Richard III Society. Bosworth Battlefield is now a tourist attraction with an excellent interpretation centre which is open in the afternoon throughout the spring and summer. There is a battle trail footpath, a model diorama, a film theatre showing the battle scene from "Richard III", an exhibition of photographs and armour, a shop and restaurant.

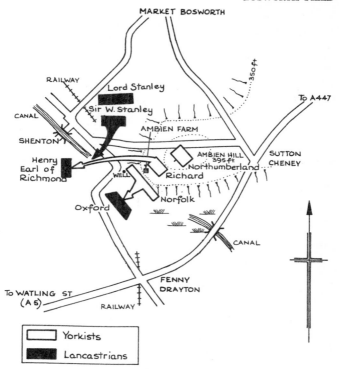

Battle of Bosworth Field, 1485

STOKE, 16 June, 1487

Nottinghamshire O/S Landranger 129 (755 495)

Just outside Newark on the south side of the Trent river is the small village of East Stoke. There is a sudden steep bank to the hill that runs at right-angles to the village. It is an ideal defensive position. After Bosworth Henry VII, the final victor for the Lancastrians, was safely on the English throne but two years later trouble broke out in Ireland. Lambert Simnel, a ten-year-old boy, was proclaimed King Edward VI by the Earl of Lincoln. The Earl was a Yorkist by birth and so wealthy that he could hire 2,000 German mercenaries to fight for him. Joined by Lord Lovell, Richard III's former Admiral, he landed on the Lancashire coast in June 1487. With Irish reinforcements and discontented northern Englishmen, the total rebel army was about 9,000. Lincoln marched east towards York, held for the King, then south towards Newark, which was also in Royal hands, so he decided to watch both the north and south approaches on the Fosse Way. Henry VII was, by then, closing in on Newark from Nottingham with about 12,000 men.

The Earl of Oxford, a veteran of Barnet and Bosworth, led the Royal vanguard, and the rest of the Royal army followed in two groups at some distance behind. Lincoln was a shrewd soldier. His line was at an angle to the road so that the opposing army would have to wheel round to get in position. When the enemy approached in columns, the German troops, well armed with crossbows, opened fire. Oxford's men fought hard but made little impression on their enemies until they were reinforced by Henry VII's second and third lines. The "beggarly, naked and almost unarmed" Irish were the first to break. Many were caught in the narrow Red Gutter, a gully down the steep slope at the west, and others were drowned in the 150-yard wide river Trent.

The battle lasted for three hours and the German troops under Schwarz fought bravely. Most of the rebel leaders were killed, in spite of Henry VII's order that Lincoln should be spared. Two of them however survived—Lambert Simnel, whom Henry made a kitchen scullion in his palace, and Lord Lovell who forced his horse into the water at Fiskerton and, so legend says, hid himself in a secret room in Minster Lovell, his Oxfordshire house. Here in 1708 a skeleton was found when a chimney was repaired. The event was described by a local historian: "sitting at a table which was before him, with a book, paper, pen, etc.; in another part of the room lay a cap ... the family and others judged this to be Lord Lovell."

Henry went to Lincoln to give thanks for his victory in the cathedral. The Yorkist cause was not quite dead. The Earl of Lincoln was one of seven brothers, sons of the late King Richard III's sister, and Henry had married a Yorkist queen who had other sisters. This battle has often been neglected in the mistaken belief that Bosworth ended the Wars of the Roses. Stoke was the real ending and the execution of the unfortunate young Earl of Warwick in 1499, the last male

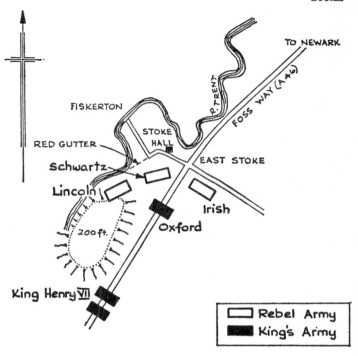

Battle of Stoke, 1487

Yorkist with a direct claim to the throne, added the finishing touch.

Stoke today:

The village is known as East Stoke and it must not be confused with the town of Stoke-on-Trent. Three miles south of Newark on A46 the river bends sharply and Stoke Hall stands a quarter of a mile from the bank. Fiskerton does not look fordable and on the map a ferry — now extinct — is marked. When exploring the ground in 1825 the owner of Stoke Hall found skeletons in Red Gutter and near the church. The road ends at Fiskerton which is a pleasant place for a picnic. There is a monument against the wall of East Stoke church.

FLODDEN, 9th September, 1513
Northumberland O/S Landranger 74 (890 370)

"No Scottish army had ever taken the field so well equipped," wrote a Scottish historian about the 40,000 men with whom King James IV crossed into England in 1513. Henry VIII had taken a large army to France and the French King, Louis XII, had called on his traditional Scottish allies for help. The young Henry had left a small army in England under the hands of the Earl of Surrey who, although over 70 and a veteran of Richard III's defeated army at Bosworth, was an experienced leader who knew the border country well. Setting out for the Tweed valley, where the Scots had captured Ford castle, Surrey collected his army *en route*. It amounted to about 26,000 men but included a large force of archers. His men at arms had short bills and halberds while the Scots had 15-foot French pikes.

At Alnwick a party of armed 'sailors' under Thomas Howard, Surrey's eldest son, joined the English army and precise instructions were given to the men on the tactics to be employed. Howard was appointed second-in-command. The Scottish army was strongly positioned on Flodden Edge near the Till river. Surrey sent Roger Croix, his herald, to King James to suggest the time and place of the forthcoming battle, but the Scots king was not prepared for this old-fashioned method and replied that he would fight when and where he chose. Undaunted, Surrey divided his army and on 9th September, in the pouring rain, moved east and circled round the Scots position crossing the Till at Twizel and Milford bridges so as to cut off the Scottish retreat.

It was a bold move and James could have caught him on the flank when his army was divided. Instead he turned his men round and took up a defensive position on Branxton hill facing north. His artillery, under Borthwick, was the most modern in Europe but he could not advance quickly without leaving it behind. The smoke from his camp fires at Flodden prevented the English from observing his movements. The English vanguard under Thomas Howard had to cross Pallin's burn in a column with bogland on either side. No sooner had they deployed than James's borderers charged. The English right wing under Edmund Howard was swept aside and Howard was wounded. The English artillery

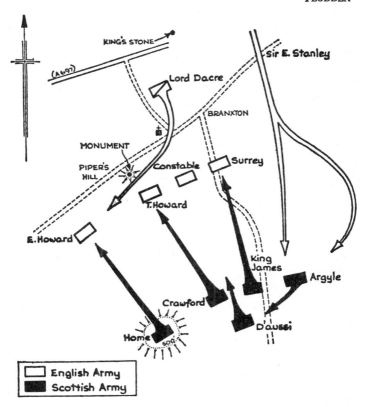

Battle of Flodden, 1513

which had crossed the bog at Sandyford now came into its own. The Scottish king formed his men into schiltrons, massed circles of pikemen round their standards, and the two centre divisions, led by Crawford and James himself, advanced on Surrey and his son. On the other side Lord Dacre, who had been stationed behind with his horsemen in reserve, attacked the Borderers in the flank and drove them off. Their leader, Lord Home, was later executed for treachery in failing to bring in his reserves against the English horse-

71

men, but his ruffians were so busy plundering the dead that he was unable to rally them.

The English rearguard under Sir Edward Stanley appeared on the flank of the unengaged Scottish division. While holding their attention with part of his force Stanley sent his archers round out of sight to fire at their flank. These Scots, mostly poorly armed Highlanders, turned and fled. Stanley now attacked the main Scottish force in the rear while Dacre charged from the right flank. James, reinforced by his French reserve under D'Aussi, fought bravely but at last a halberd thrust killed him. It was victory for the English halberd over the unwieldy pike and heavy sword. Five thousand Scots including their king and three bishops were slaughtered. The Earl of Surrey, who had been mocked by the Scots as "the old crooked Earl in a chariot" because his gout forced him to travel by coach, regained his Norfolk dukedom and henceforward Henry VIII had no more trouble with Scotland.

Flodden today:

A simple stone monument to the dead of both nations marks the site of the battle. To get to it take the A697 from Morpeth north to Coldstream and turn off before the Tweed bridge to the village of Branxton. The monument is on a small hill above the church and the view around is outstanding. There is an interpretation board by the monument.

NEWBURN FORD, 28th August, 1640
Northumberland O/S Landranger 88 (165 652)

The reign of Charles I was beset with difficulties from the first and in Scotland the new prayer-book of Archbishop Laud led to the signing of the Covenant and the first Bishop's War. Charles captured Scottish ships in English ports and sent Sir Jacob Astley to fortify Newcastle. Berwick and Hull were similarly fortified but loyal Edinburgh castle was captured by the Scots in March 1639. The Scots had a capable, experienced general, Sir Alexander Leslie, formerly field marshal to Gustavus Adolphus, who trained his men to fight in brigades with musketeers supporting the pikemen. His one weak arm was his cavalry but his artillery was very effective and, apart from heavy cannon, he developed a German idea of making temporary cannon, two of which could be carried on a single

14. Edgecote, 1469: Edgecote House and church.

15. Barnet, 1471: the monument at Hadley Green.

16. *Tewkesbury, 1471: Bloody Meadow.*

17. *Tewkesbury, 1471: Gupshill Manor.*

18. *Bosworth Field, 1485: King Richard's Well.*

19. *Bosworth Field, 1485: the memorial in King Richard's Field.*

20. Stoke, 1487: the memorial at East Stoke church.

TO COMMEMORATE
THE DEAD AT STOKE FIELD
16TH JUNE 1487.

JOHN DE LA POLE
EARL OF LINCOLN
SIR THOMAS GERALDINE
COL. MARTIN SCHWARTZ
AND 7000 OTHERS
ENGLISH IRISH AND GERMAN

21. Stoke, 1487: modern banners hanging in the chancel.

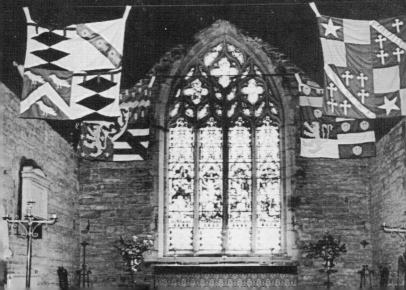

22. Flodden, 1513: the battlefield from the monument.

23. Flodden, 1513: the inscription on the monument.

FLODDEN
1513
TO THE BRAVE OF BOTH NATIONS
ERECTED 1910

24. Edgehill, 1642: the tower at the Castle Inn.

25. Edgehill, 1642: the battlefield from Edgehill.

26. Edgehill, 1642: the monument to the battle.

27. *Chalgrove Field, 1643: the Hampden monument.*

28. *Adwalton Moor, 1643: the battlefield.*

packhorse. The barrels, of small calibre, were made from bar iron, bound in hide.

The First Scots War ended in an uneasy truce at Berwick. The Second started when Leslie regiments crossed the Tweed in August 1640. Lord Conway, who had been attempting to fortify Newcastle, hastily built two sconces at Newburn, a few miles east of the town, where there were two fords accessible only at low tide. The English army had a small mutiny when two pence were deducted from the pay of each man for accoutrements. Lord Conway, nevertheless, had 3,000 foot and 1,500 horse to hold up Leslie's Scots until reinforcements could arrive from the King at York.

On the night of 27th August Leslie was at Heddon Law looking down over Conway's position. The latter had placed his artillery in the two sconces, one of which was commanded by Colonel Lunsford. When a Scots officer appeared the following day to water his horse he was shot down by an English bullet and the battle started. Leslie had placed some of his portable cannon on the tower of Newburn church. These were skilfully managed and the shot bowled into Lunsford's earthworks killing many soldiers and forcing the rest to flee in disorder.

Lord Hope's son led his volunteers from the Edinburgh law courts across the river, which was just fordable at four o'clock. Then Colonel Blair's musketeers crossed, followed by the Scottish horse. Conway's second sconce was now abandoned and the foot retired in disorder. Young Wilmot, in command of the cavalry, charged the Scottish lifeguards of Sir Thomas Hope's regiment. The Scots yielded and only Blair's flank fire prevented them from being driven back into the river. Lord Wilmot was wounded and captured and Lord Conway's standard-bearer, Charles Porter, was killed and the standard captured. About fifty were killed on both sides and the fleeing English cavalry trampled down some of their own infantry in a narrow lane. Had someone been able to re-organise them the Scots might still have been defeated, for only part of General Leslie's army made the crossing, the tide allowing a mere one and a half hours to cross.

Conway fled to Durham and Newcastle was abandoned. 'Never so many ran from so few,' said one writer. Even Vicar Alvey made a hasty retreat on the back of a horse, 'without waiting for a cushion'. The Mayor surrendered to a company of Douglas's horsemen on Saturday 30th August and it was not until August 1641, after being paid £60,000, that Leslie retired to Scotland.

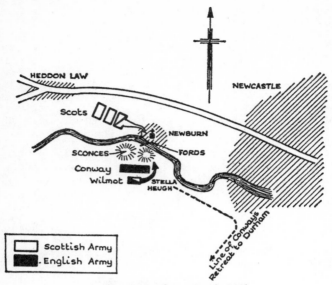

Battle of Newburn Ford, 1640

Newburn Ford today:

Best approached from the A69 north of the river, Newburn is an industrial suburb of Newcastle. The river was altered in the nineteenth century so nothing remains of the fords, one of which ran diagonally across the river near the present bridge. There is a tumulus at Ryton church but it may well date from another era. The Stella breastworks were visible until about 1917. In the Black `Gate museum, Newcastle, there is a cart wheel found at Newburn, no doubt from a cart which did not make the crossing in time.

EDGEHILL, 23 October, 1642
Warwickshire O/S Landranger 151 (357 492)

Bosworth was the last major battle to be fought in England between two English armies until the Civil War and in the intervening one hundred and fifty-seven years much change had taken place in warfare. Armour, apart from helmets and

82

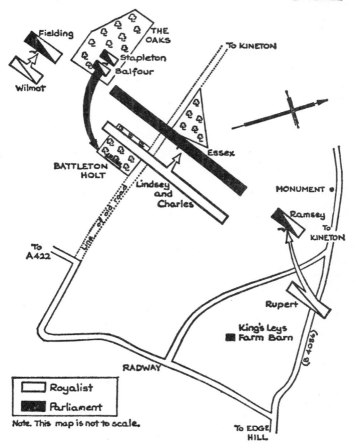

Battle of Edgehill, 1642

breast-plates, was abandoned; infantry was armed with pikes and with muskets, some so heavy that they had to be fired on a crutch support; heavy cannon were introduced on the field, as were small sakers that fired grape-shot, and there were numerous other field guns. But more important than the artillery was the cavalry, armed with pistols and swords.

83

The old idea of battle was the 'caracole'. This involved a brisk trot to about 50 yards from the enemy line, a barrage of pistols then a swift retreat to make way for a barrage from the second line of horse. There was little contact or actual sword fighting. Prince Rupert introduced the Swedish method of Gustavus Adolphus. Not all his men had pistols and he told them to bunch together and gallop through the enemy position using pistols and swords only at close range.

When sides were taken in the Civil War King Charles I found support amongst a majority of the House of Lords and just over a third of the Commons, the majority of the country gentry, the Catholics and the universities. The Puritans, the expanding trading classes, the City of London and the Royal Navy supported Parliament. The closing of the ports to foreign aid weighted the scales heavily against the King from the outset.

Geographically the poorer parts of the country, i.e. the northern counties, Wales and the West Country, supported the King, while Parliament's strength lay in the eastern counties south of the Humber, southern England, the cloth districts of the West Riding and Somerset, and all main seaports.

Both sides secured generals who had some experience of war. Parliamentary leaders were Robert Devereux, Earl of Essex, Sir William Waller and the Earl of Manchester and, later, Sir Thomas Fairfax and Oliver Cromwell. The King was served by his brilliant nephew Prince Rupert of the Palatinate in Germany (who could probably have won the war if he had been allowed to), Sir Ralph Hopton, Lord Goring and the Duke of Newcastle.

Both armies were initially badly organised. There was a reluctance of local levies to leave their counties unprotected and on the Royalist side there was too much concentration on the maintenance of small scattered garrisons. To begin with the King had the great advantage of superb cavalry contributed by the nobility, while Parliament had the only reasonably competent infantry in the country, the London Trained Bands.

Charles I, having raised his standard at Nottingham in August 1642, proceeded to Shrewsbury collecting troops. The Parliamentary army under the Earl of Essex moved out of London towards Nottingham and Charles moved to Chester, Prince Rupert going on to Worcester where he defeated a force of Roundhead cavalry at Powick Bridge. The Earl of Essex reached Worcester and Charles, inspired by Rupert's success, blocked his retreat at Edgehill. The hill rises 600 feet for three miles in a boomerang shape, the long arm looking over towards the Kineton plain, the rear overlooking the Warwick-Stratford road and Essex's route to London. It was and still is a commanding spot.

Charles had over 13,000 men, Essex slightly less. With Rupert on the right wing facing Ramsey's horse and Wilmot facing Fielding's horse on the left, it was like a football line-up. Essex, however, had placed a cavalry reserve under Balfour, a capable Scottish soldier, and Stapleton, in a wood behind his infantry. The Royalists had descended from the hill before the battle and when Rupert charged, the impetus of his horse and his superiority in numbers meant that he carried all before him. Wilmot met with similar success on the other flank and a chase to Kineton and beyond developed.

The infantry in the centre fought behind hedges, neither side gaining ground until Balfour's cavalry charged the centre regiment, cutting through them and sweeping into Battleton Holt, a small copse where the Royalist heavy guns were positioned. There was no means of capturing the guns so Balfour contented himself with cutting their traces and killing the gunners. The Roundhead line now wheeled to the right and a great hand-to-hand fight took place round the Royal standard which was captured, Sir Edmund Verney being killed and Charles's general, the Earl of Lindsey, mortally wounded. The King was now in difficulties and only the weariness of the enemy and the reappearance of some of the cavalry prevented his retreat. One of the returning horsemen, Captain John Smith, saw a group of Balfour's men making off with the standard. He charged them alone, killing one with his sword and wounding another. The rest fled and the Royal standard was returned to the King. Captain Smith was knighted the following morning.

Charles spent the night in Kings Leys farm barn, his troops remaining in their positions. Essex collected his men with difficulty and withdrew next day to Warwick and the road to London was open for Charles who entered Oxford, his headquarters for the remainder of the war, in triumph.

The first campaign of the war now took the form of a race between the armies of Charles and Essex for London, but Charles delayed his march on London too long and although Rupert's advance guard captured Brentford, the combined forces of Essex, who had not delayed, and the trained bands of London waiting at Turnham Green forced the King to withdraw to winter quarters in Oxford.

Edgehill today:

Leave Banbury by A41 to Warwick. Turn left after about 6½ miles on B4086. Continue down the hill towards Kineton (pronounced Kine-ton). There is a small monument on the left of the road half a mile after a level crossing. The battlefield itself is W.D. property and is covered in ugly brick bunkers. The steep hill is impressive, although in 1642 there were no trees on the ridge. The view from the top of Castle Inn gives one the best impression of Charles's view on the morning of the battle.

There is little to see on the ground but there is a battlefield museum in the stable block of nearby Farnborough Park, open to the public in the summer.

STRATTON, 16th May, 1643
Cornwall O/S Landranger 190 (072 229)

The Battle of Braddock Down in January 1643 established the Royalists in Cornwall. Sir Ralph Hopton defeated Colonel Ruthin largely because of a gallant charge by Sir Bevil Grenville's Cornish foot. However, Plymouth was strongly held by Parliament and the Cornish trained bands decided not to cross the border into Devon, and so, with Plymouth supplied by sea, it looked like stalemate.

On 22nd April, after a temporary period of truce, James Chudleigh, the 25-year-old son of Sir George Chudleigh, took command of the Parliamentary forces from the Earl of Stamford who was sick with gout. He had over 2,000 men and decided to attack Launceston, where Hopton was drawn up with about 1,200. Throughout the day the Parliamentarians tried to attack the bridge but Hopton was reinforced and eventually turned the tide and pursued Chudleigh to Okehampton. At night the Royalist advance was ambushed on Sourton Down and 1,000 muskets were captured together with Hopton's correspondence. The latter then withdrew to Launceston and on 15th May Stamford, now recovered, crossed the Cornish border at Stratton, sending Sir George Chudleigh and the Parliamentary horse to Bodmin to interrupt a muster of Royalist trained bands. Camped on a hill near Stratton, now known as Stamford Hill, the Earl imagined himself in an impregnable position, but events were to prove otherwise.

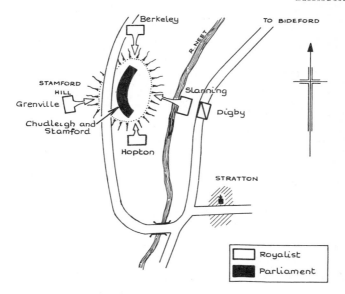

Battle of Stratton, 1643

Hopton, whose army was reduced to about 3,000, decided to get in between Chudleigh and the Earl. He camped outside Stratton and early on the 16th advanced on the hill, which was fortified with cannon and an earthwork. He divided his army into four groups under Grenville on the south-west, Slanning on the east, his own group on the south and Digby with the cavalry on the east as well as protecting the road from which the Parliamentary horse was expected. The Royalists could make no impression on the Earl's position and by three in the afternoon they were left with scarcely four barrels of powder.

Concealing his shortage of powder from his men, Hopton gave the order for a general charge with pike and sword alone on four sides. The few remaining Parliamentary horse under Stamford escaped and James Chudleigh rallied his foot to push Grenville and Berkeley back down the hill but pressed on too far and was captured. In forty-five minutes the four parties had met on the hill and the remaining Parliamentarians were put to flight by their own cannon. 1,700 were captured

87

with all the baggage, including £5,000 and seventy barrels of powder.

Stratton was one of the most remarkable victories of the Civil War for either side. The Cornish infantry and their commanders proved invincible and such was their effect on young Chudleigh that he changed sides and a few weeks later his father resigned his Parliamentary commission. Hopton joined forces with Prince Maurice in June at Chard. Sir John Berkeley, who escaped to the Continent and became head of the Duke of York's household, was raised to the peerage as Baron Berkeley of Stratton. His companion Sir Bevil Grenville fought on to July 1643 when he met a legendary soldier's death at Lansdown (see page 92).

Stratton today:

The village of Stratton lies a few miles inland from Bude on the north coast. There are earthworks still visible on the hill and a monument to the battle on the side of a building.

CHALGROVE FIELD, 18th June, 1643
Oxfordshire O/S Landranger 165 (644 971)

Chalgrove today is almost suburban, but behind the new houses Chalgrove field is still undeveloped and Hampden's monument, erected in the nineteenth century, looks down on the place where he saw his last fight.

On 17th June 1643 Prince Rupert at Oxford received a message from a Roundhead deserter, Colonel Hurry, that a convoy was *en route* for Thame from London with £21,000 for the payment of Essex's army. Rupert left for High Wycombe via Chislehampton Bridge with 1,000 cavalry and 500 foot. He arrived too late (the convoy was hidden in a wood) so he turned on Chinnor, set fire to it and captured about 120 Parliamentary recruits.

John Hampden was at Watlington with a small group of horsemen and realising that Rupert could be cut off he sent a message to Essex at Thame and with scarcely 200 men he followed Rupert's route towards Chislehampton Bridge. "This insolence", said Rupert, "is not to be borne", and, halting his men in a cornfield at Chalgrove, he arranged his cavalry in front with their pistols loaded. Hampden, reinforced by some of Essex's dragoons, led the charge across the corn. The Royalists held their fire until the last moment when a close

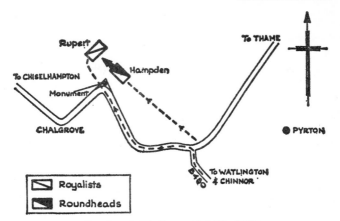

Battle of Chalgrove Field, 1643

barrage from pistols and carbines followed by a charge drove the outnumbered Parliamentarians in all directions. Struck twice in the shoulder, "with his head hanging down and resting his hands upon the neck of his horse", Hampden rode away towards his wife's home at Pyrton.

It was late and Pyrton was not safe, so escorted by his lifelong friend Arthur Goodwin, he travelled to Thame where he was attended by surgeons and a Dr Gyles, sent by the King. Dr Gyles lived at Chinnor parsonage and Hampden had helped design his house before the war. On 24th June Hampden died in a house not far from the Grammar School he had attended forty years before. Today his statue stands not only in Aylesbury's old market place but in the National Liberal Club, although he probably never stood in such a position with his sword drawn and arm outstretched (at Chalgrove he was mounted with a pistol). His death was a shattering blow to Parliament. "I would we could all aly (admit) to it to heart", wrote his friend Goodwin, "that God takes away the best amongst us."

Chalgrove today:

If you ignore the new houses, this is one of the least changed battlefields of the Civil War. It still has standing corn in June. Turn left off the A40 after leaving High Wycombe and go towards Oxford on the B4009 to Watlington. Turn right on to the B480 and the Hampden monument is at a road junction. The names of subscribers to the monument are interesting; four of the Fiennes family fought for Parliament for instance, and there are other names well-known in 1643.

ADWALTON MOOR, 30th June, 1643
Yorkshire O/S Landranger 104 (222 283)

In 1643 the Civil War in Yorkshire developed into a struggle between the Fairfaxes, father and son, who held Leeds, Bradford and the recently captured Wakefield, and Lord Newcastle's Royalists, who had been strengthened by the arrival earlier in the year of fresh armaments from abroad when the Queen's ships put into Bridlington.

At the end of June Newcastle with nearly 10,000 men set out to storm Howley House, home of the Parliamentary Lord Savile near Pontefract. He then moved on Bradford, determined to secure the West Riding for the King and to forge a safe passage for the Queen's small army to get through to Oxford.

On 30th June Sir Thomas Fairfax's cavalry and his father's infantry moved out of Bradford, which was ill provisioned for a siege, and took up a position on Adwalton Moor blocking the approach road from Leeds. In number they were about 5,000 but, apart from the local clubmen, they were better armed than the Royalists. Newcastle had two heavy guns, Gog and Magog, with him and he spread his large army out on the moor so that it outflanked the hard-pressed Parliamentary forces. The Forlorn Hope positioned on Westgate Hill was commanded by Sir Robert Clavering of Callaly Castle. It consisted of dragoons, horse and foot raised at his own expense from Northumberland. The Fairfaxes held their ground but Lord Gifford's left flank was charged by a regiment of pikemen under Colonel Kirton, of the famous Whitecoats regiment. It faltered and gave way. At the same time a troop of horse made their way round to the rear of Fairfax's centre. The luckless Sir Thomas fled to Halifax and the remains of Gifford and Lord Fairfax's men retreated to Bradford where they were attacked the following day. The Royalists lost a few men including Colonel Heron, whose body was stripped by four Roundheads, whom Lord Fairfax noted were all killed by a single shot from one of the Royalist guns shortly after their misdeed. The Roundheads lost 500 men killed, three guns and 1,400 prisoners.

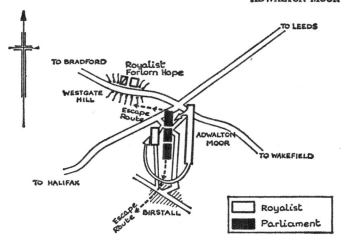

Battle of Adwalton Moor, 1643

After forty hours in the saddle Lord Fairfax reached Hull, but his son, whose wife was captured by Newcastle, lost most of his men in his escape when they were intercepted at Selby. Newcastle charitably sent Lady Fairfax in his own coach to her husband. The Queen with 3,000 infantry and 30 troops of horse rode into Oxford and the Royalists, after unsuccessfully besieging Hull, retreated to York where the following year Black Tom joined with Cromwell and had his revenge at Marston Moor

Adwalton Moor today:

The moor is a large green at the junction of the A50 and A282. The area is industrial but the lane from Oakwell to Cleckheaton and Halifax which was taken by Sir Thomas in his retreat still exists and it was probably the top part of this route which was used by Newcastle to send his attacking force to strike Lord Fairfax in the rear. Clavering's regiment was presumably stationed on Westgate Hill to cut off the retreat to Bradford, which they failed to do, although Lord Fairfax and Gifford may have used a different route in their escape.

LANSDOWN, 6th July, 1643

Somerset O/S Landranger 172 (725 705)

The victory at Stratton ensured the advance of the Cornish Royalists into Devon and Somerset. When their army left Chard on 4th June it consisted of 4,000 foot, 500 horse, 300 dragoons and 21 guns. It was commanded by Prince Maurice, Hopton and the Marquis of Hertford. The headstrong Maurice became involved in a cavalry skirmish at Chewton Mendip, ignoring Hopton's advice to withdraw; he was wounded and captured for a time.

The Parliamentary army had no split comand, for Sir William Waller had secured Bath and been reinforced by Haselrig's 500 'Lobsters' (see Roundway Down, page 94). He took up a position on Claverton Down—near the present university—and Hopton sent some of his foot to secure the bridge near Batheaston but during the night of 3rd July Waller crossed over the valley in Bath and occupied Lansdown ridge and in the morning opened fire on the Royalist position. Hopton took his army back to Tog Hill via Marshfield. On the afternoon of the 5th Hopton ordered a retreat back to Marshfield and seeing this, Waller sent down Haselrig with 400 horse to attack the Royalist rear. The Cornish foot stood fast and beat them back and then Sir Bevil Grenville's regiment led the charge up the hill in the face of terrible musket fire. Every piece of cover was used including a stone wall which gave Grenville's men some much needed shelter. They were supported by Hertford's and Carnarvon's horse.

Five cavalry charges were beaten off and eventually some of the guns were dragged up the hill and the Parliamentarians retreated. In the moment of victory Sir Bevil was poleaxed leading a cavalry attack and, according to legend, the giant Payne, his servant, put the thirteen-year-old John Grenville on his father's horse and led the final charge on Waller's position. Darkness prevented further fighting. In the morning Hopton discovered that Waller had retreated to Bath and that he had won the day at great cost, almost entirely because of the bravery of the Cornish foot. Many of his cavalry had fled; as Slingsby, one of his commanders, said, 'Had our horse been as good as the enemy's, the rebels had never gone off the field unharmed.' Lansdown was a temporary victory and it was to be at another action, at Roundway Down, that the Royalist horse were to redeem themselves.

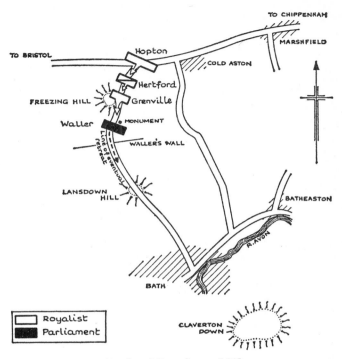

Battle of Lansdown, 1643

Lansdown today:

The monument to Sir Bevil Grenville can be found at the left of the road up Lansdown from the A420 Chippenham-Bristol road. Further on, where the Ordnance Survey map marks 'earthwork' is a stone wall that may have been the final position of the Parliamentary troops. Waller placed pikes behind this wall and lit torches to deceive Hopton that he was still there before retreating to Bath. From many aspects the battlefield is not very different from what it must have looked like in 1643.

93

ROUNDWAY DOWN, 13th July, 1643
Wiltshire O/S Landranger 173 (017 655)

During 1643 fighting went on all over England. The Royalist army in the west was very successful and Sir Ralph Hopton's victory at Lansdown Hill, although a near thing, forced Waller back to Bath. The Royalists moved to Devizes and Prince Maurice, dodging a Roundhead patrol, went to Oxford for reinforcements. Hopton, blinded by an accidental explosion after Lansdown, was so short of ammunition that he had to make some out of resin and bed cord. His men were weary and badly armed, numbering about 2,500, but Maurice's relieving cavalry numbered 1,800 and had two small guns. Waller, who had gathered reinforcements in Bath, had about 3,000 foot and 2,000 horse, equally weary but better disciplined. They included Sir Arthur Haselrig's 'Lobsters', musketeers in close-fitting armour which was virtually sword proof, and a few cannon.

On 13th July Waller heard of the approach of Maurice, Byron and Wilmot. Hopton's men were still in Devizes but Wilmot, who took command as the senior cavalry officer, charged the Roundhead cavalry which was drawn up on a steep hill near Roundway village. Waller was taken by surprise for his infantry found no opposing infantry to fight and could not fire at the cavalry for fear of hitting their own men. Haselrig's tin men had time for one stand before they were driven down the steep hill. Waller's cavalry tried to escape through a gap by Beacon Hill only to find a 300-foot precipice, down which most of them fell.

Meanwhile Hopton's Cornish infantry, warned in advance by Wilmot's gun signal, climbed out of Devizes and fell on the leaderless Roundhead infantry. Over 600 were killed, about twice that number wounded and captured together with all Waller's guns, ammunition and baggage. It was an amazing victory and even a Parliamentary officer remarked: "We must needs look upon this as the hand of our God mightily against us, for it was He only that made us fly."

The Royalist tide now reached its peak. On 26th July Rupert captured Bristol and the western garrisons all fell to the Cavaliers apart from Lyme and Poole. In Kent, where there was very little action in the Civil War, a Royalist rising threatened London, where the hand of Pym was losing control. But Royalists in the north, east and west were reluctant to converge on London while Hull, Plymouth and Gloucester

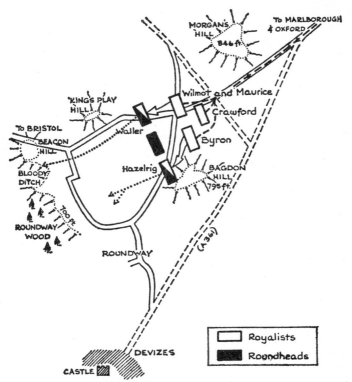

Battle of Roundway Down, 1643

were in Roundhead hands so Charles tried to encourage them and open the road to south Wales by laying siege to Gloucester. Realising the psychological importance of this city's resistance, the Earl of Essex and the London Militia set out to relieve it. "Run-away Down" had been a significant victory but the forces taking part were too small for it to have any lasting effect on the war.

Roundway Down today:

Take the A361 from Swindon to Devizes and Roundway is the village up the hill to the right just before Devizes. The land is cultivated now except for Morgan's Hill and its adjacent golf course. The best view of the site is from King's Play Hill, which is reached from Heddington village near Calne. Beacon Hill slopes are still as steep as in 1643. Bagdon Hill (now called Roundway Hill) and Morgan's Hill flank the position of Waller's army. The roads are mere tracks but there is a picnic site overlooking Bloody Ditch where Waller's cavalry came to grief.

NEWBURY I, 20th September, 1643

Berkshire O/S Landranger 174 (455 652)

After the Battle of Roundway Down, Bristol fell to the Royalists and in the west only Colonel Massey at Gloucester held out for Parliament. In August Charles laid siege to the town and in London Essex assembled a large army to go to Massey's relief. It consisted mostly of the London Trained Bands who, mostly untrained, were raised to defend London and paid for by the City. The siege was withdrawn and both sides moved south towards the capital, heading towards Newbury. Charles reached the town first, bivouacked across Essex's path and brought him to battle the following day.

Prince Rupert intercepted Essex's cavalry at Aldbourne Chase and pushed him off the London road, which passed through Newbury. On 19th September the Royalist army occupied the town and Essex camped two miles to the south at Enborne. The land between the Kennet river and the En brook was more enclosed than it is today. Commanding the whole position is a four hundred foot spur near Wash farm. The Royalists sent to occupy this were exhausted and spent the night in the farm instead. In the morning Essex's artillery opened up from the hill so that Sir Nicholas Byron's foot below were forced to shelter behind a hedge. His nephew, Lord Byron, was given the order to clear the hill, which after three charges he succeeded in doing, only to lose most of the ground later in the day.

In the first charge young Lucius Cary, Lord Falkland, Charles's Secretary of State, was killed. His replacement, Lord Digby, was unreliable and had more influence over the King in the fatal years to come.

"The battle", according to a Cavalier witness, "was a kind of hedge fight, neither army was drawn out into the field, if it had it would never have lasted from six in the morning till ten at night." The Royalist right wing gained some ground and Skippon's men on Parliament's right wing gained the high ground. The young Earl of Carnarvon was killed by a cannon

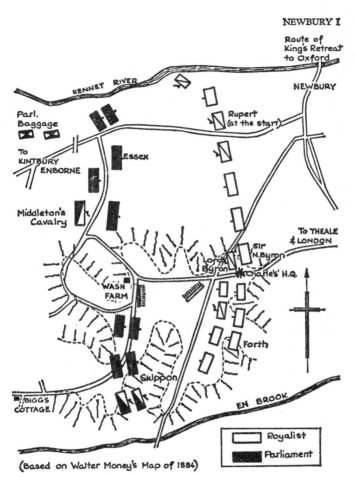

Route of
King's Retreat
to Oxford

KENNET RIVER

NEWBURY

Parl.
Baggage

Rupert
(at the start)

To
KINTBURY
ENBORNE

Essex

Middleton's
Cavalry

To THEALE
& LONDON

Sir
N. Byron

Lord
Byron

Charles' H.Q.

WASH
FARM

Forth

BIGGS
COTTAGE

Skippon

EN BROOK

Royalist

Parliament

(Based on Walter Money's Map of 1884)

First Battle of Newbury, 1643

shot and the Earl of Sunderland also met his death. At night-
fall the Royalists, perhaps due to their twenty guns using so
much ammunition, retired into Newbury and the infantry
returned to Oxford, desperately short of powder. Essex was
left to continue his march to London, his army badly depleted,
for out of about 10,000 on each side at least 6,000 were dead

or wounded. "All were Englishmen," wrote the Buckingham-shire Roundhead, Bulstrode Whitelocke, "and pity it was that such courage should be spent in blood of each other."

The following day Prince Rupert could not resist another charge and the Parliamentary rear were caught unawares near Theale when a squadron of cavalry bore down on them from a narrow lane. In the struggle that followed, Sir Philip Staple-ton, finding himself suddenly surrounded, rode up to Rupert and fired his pistol at point blank range. It failed to go off and thus ended the most confused and one of the bloodiest battles of the Civil War. As he had failed to destroy the Parliamentary army, Charles could not attempt to take Lon-don and contented himself with retaking Reading after Essex withdrew.

Newbury today:

Leave the town by the Andover road. Half-way up the hill is the monument to Lord Falkland opposite the Gun Inn. This was Charles's H.Q. Turn right and all the streets have names connected with the battle. The road bends left at Wash Farm. Continue down the hill beyond the bridge and on the left is the thatched Bigg's Cottage where Essex spent the night before the battle. There is a stone to the fallen on one of the two tumuli on Wash Common but the mounds themselves were there before the battle.

WINCEBY, 11th October, 1643

Lincolnshire O/S Landranger 122 (315 689)

In 1642 the first campaign of the Civil War was a race for the possession of London. The battle of Edgehill left the way open for Charles I but he delayed too long while establish-ing his headquarters at Oxford and he was turned back at Turnham Green. In 1643 fighting went on all over England. The ubiquitous Prince Rupert scored at Chalgrove Field in Oxfordshire in June. In the West the Royalists won a series of successes culminating in July at Roundway Down, and only Gloucester held for Parliament.

On 30th June 1643 the Roundheads were beaten by New-castle at Adwalton Moor near Bradford and the Fairfaxes, father and son, were surrounded in Hull. Meanwhile the Parliamentary forces in the eastern counties under the Earl of Manchester were being drilled into shape by Colonel Oliver

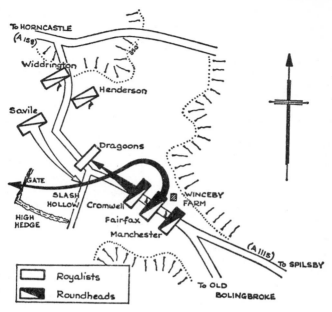

Battle of Winceby, 1643

Cromwell. By September he had ten troops of horse tried successfully at Grantham and Gainsborough. On 26th September Cromwell crossed the Humber in a boat, in spite of Newcastle's army, and returned later in the day with Sir Thomas Fairfax and about 500 cavalry, which he managed to ferry across the river. Meanwhile a Royalist rising in King's Lynn had been put down by the Earl of Manchester, who moved towards the Royalist-held castle at Bolingbroke, which is about fifteen miles north of Boston in Lincolnshire.

Newcastle now decided to act. He relieved Gainsborough and sent orders for the Newark commander, a Scottish veteran soldier, Sir John Henderson, to relieve Bolingbroke Castle. With Sir William Widdrington's troops from Lincoln and Gainsborough, the Royalist force numbered about 2,500. Manchester, Cromwell and Fairfax had about 2,000 cavalry with a small detachment of foot.

Credit for the victory at Winceby is often given to Cromwell but Fairfax was the real hero. Henderson, who had

99

positioned himself on a ridge, sent his dragoons forward towards the Roundheads drawn up on the opposite ridge near Winceby Farm. When Cromwell charged, the dragoons' second volley killed his horse and when he had found a replacement, the battle was almost over. Fairfax with the second troop moved on to the right hand ridge—it was a horseshoe shape rather like that at Cheriton—and attacked diagonally across the field. The Royalist right wing under Savile, caught on the flank, turned and fled. Many of them were trapped in a field with a high hedge and gate that opened inwards where they were mercilessly cut down by Fairfax's troopers. The place is now called Slash Hollow.

Henderson had no option but to retreat. Manchester described the action later: "Our men had little else to do but to pursue a flying enemy which they did for many miles." Hull was relieved on the same day after a high tide had flooded the siege works and a sortie led by Fairfax senior had surprised the besieged. Newcastle was compelled to draw his main force back to York. The victory raised the reputation of Cromwell and the Eastern Horse, but it also convinced the Parliamentary leaders that when the New Model Army was formed, the man to lead it was Thomas Fairfax.

Winceby today:

Most maps do not show Winceby, which consists of a manor, a farm and a large Georgian house on the A115 from Horncastle to Spilsby near the junction with the A158, which is the main road to Skegness. The horseshoe-shaped ridge is now crossed by the main road and the land is less enclosed than it was in 1643. In Horncastle church are some old pikes and the monument to Sir Ingram Hopton, a Royalist, killed in the battle "in an attempt of seizing the Arch-rebel". There is another monument to the Rev. Thomas Gibson, who was forced out of Horncastle by the Earl of Manchester but returned in 1660 "at the head of several hundreds of his friends"

NEWARK, 21 March, 1644
Nottinghamshire O/S Landranger 121 (802 555)

Both sides in the Civil War were anxious for outside help. When Charles negotiated a truce with the Irish to release English forces in Ireland, it was universally (and inaccurately) believed that Irish Catholic soldiers would also join him. The

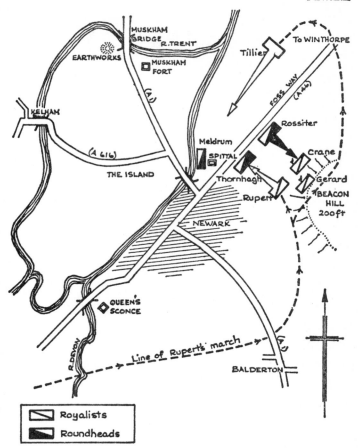

Battle of Newark, 1644

fear prompted the "Solemn League and Covenant" of Parliament with the Scots; Scots forces came in exchange for a Presbyterian Church in England.

When the Scots invaded early in 1644 Newcastle, who had fallen back on York after Winceby, found himself besieged, both by the Scots and the Roundheads from Hull, and outnumbered.

101

Charles I soon realised the importance of the town of Newark. It was on the Foss Way and the Governor, Sir Richard Byron, with his garrison in the castle could protect the York-Oxford road which was vital to Newcastle's supplies. Early in March 1644 Parliament sent Sir John Meldrum with a force of about 6,500 men to take this vital town.

Rupert, who was training new recruits at Shrewsbury, was ordered by Charles to march to its relief. Lord Byron came to his aid with the stragglers of the Royalist army that had been defeated by Fairfax at Nantwich. For infantry Rupert had two new regiments released by the truce from Ireland, under Colonel Tillier, an experienced officer. These he ferried down the Severn to Bridgnorth, where he met them with his cavalry and escorted them to Wolverhampton where 300 troops from Dudley Castle brought the small army up to about 6,000, more than half of which were cavalry.

Approaching Newark from the south-west, Rupert spent the night of 20th March at Bingham on the Nottingham-Grantham road. Newark was well protected by the rivers Trent and Devon and two forts on the Foss Way, the Spittal and the Queen's Sconce. The Trent to the north-east of the town forms an island. Here Meldrum had his headquarters and his cavalry under Sir Miles Hobart was in the Spittal, which was connected to the island by a bridge of boats. Rupert left Bingham at 2 a.m. and marching through Balderton occupied Beacon Hill. Meldrum's scouts had seen his approach and the Roundheads were drawn up in two groups with the cavalry in front. Rupert left Gerard's horse as a reserve and sent Tillier to Winthorpe to attack the vital bridge of boats. He gave his right wing to Sir Richard Crane and led his left in a valiant charge against Thornhagh's Horse who were facing him. On the other flank Colonel Rossiter, who later distinguished himself with Cromwell's horse at Naseby, led a charge up the hill where he routed Gerard's reserve, capturing Gerard himself.

Meldrum now retreated into the island, his guns keeping Tillier's infantry from the bridge. Rupert, whose charge had been successful, heard from a prisoner that Meldrum's supplies were low and decided to starve out his enemy. Byron in Newark led a surprise attack against Muskham fort, which was abandoned and after his Norfolk regiment had mutinied, Meldrum decided to surrender. Over 3,000 muskets and 11 guns were captured and many valuable supplies for the town were obtained. Meldrum's army marched out with their colours and drums but little else. Rupert's victory came at a fortunate time and more than compensated for Royalist defeats at Nantwich and Winceby. His use of river transport for his infantry was novel as well as rewarding for so often during the Civil War the foot had to march long distances and were then made to fight on the same day.

Later in the Civil War, Newark held out for the King in a long siege, finally capitulating in May 1646.

Newark today:

Situated on A1 between Stamford and Doncaster, Newark is more famous for its siege (6th March 1645 to 8th May 1646) than its battle. The actual site of the Spittal is now covered by railway lines, but the Queen's Sconce is well preserved and there are other visible earthworks at Muskham bridge, Crankley Lane, Crankley Point and Wiverton Hall. The remarkably detailed account of the siege *Newark on Trent, The Civil War and Siegeworks*, HMSO 1964, even mentions one John Tredway who supplied the Royalist garrison with leather and tobacco, and in the siege 'he was there in person to sell them'. Newark Museum has some interesting Civil War relics.

CHERITON, 29th March, 1644
Hampshire O/S Landranger 185 (598 295)

At the beginning of 1644 the Royalist army under Lord Hopton had been driven out of Sussex into Hampshire. After a skirmish at Alton in which the Royalists under Colonel Bolle were outnumbered and surrounded in the church, the Parliamentary army of about 8,500 under Waller attacked the Royalists at Arundel Castle, which was soon surrendered. Many of its defenders subsequently enlisted in Waller's army where the pay was regular and spirits were high.

From Oxford, Charles sent the Earl of Forth with 2,000 men to Winchester, where he joined the dispirited Hopton. On failing to take Basing House, near Basingstoke, Waller sent his cavalry under Balfour to Hinton Ampner and followed with his guns and infantry—an army of about 1,000 more than Hopton's force. The Royalist army camped on a horseshoe-shaped ridge between Alresford and Cheriton on 28th March, planning to attack Waller the next day. The guns were placed at the toe of the ridge and a small detachment under Lisle was on the southern part.

On 29th March Waller attacked through Cheriton Wood but Hopton's men lined the hedges and fired with such deadly

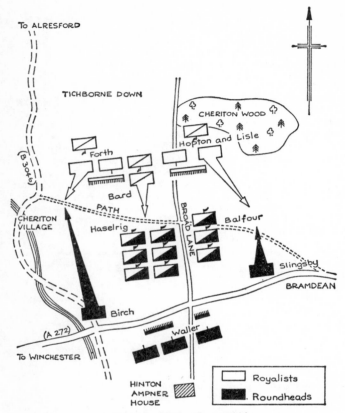

Battle of Cheriton, 1644

effect that when the Roundheads came through the wood they ran into the Royalist guns, which, firing from point blank range, did a lot of damage. Hopton won the first round, but suddenly a troop of his horse under Colonel Bard charged the enemy horse in the field below. They were surrounded by Haselrig's 'Lobsters', so called for their armour, and all killed or captured. The rest of the Royalist cavalry now attacked, one regiment at a time, and met with heavy fire. The King's cousin, Lord Stuart, was killed and the popular Sir John

Smith mortally wounded. He was the man who had rescued the colours at Edgehill and his regiment made amends for his death by killing the 'Lobster' who had shot him.

Colonel Birch on Waller's left wing now outflanked the Royalists who were forced back to Alresford. The town was burnt from one end to the other and in the chaos all the Royalist guns, save two, the baggage and the infantry escaped to Winchester. Hopton and Forth, whose divided leadership had been partly the cause of the defeat, went to Basing House. Waller was suddenly a hero, the London peace party was broken and in the words of Sir William Balfour it was "a great victory over our enemies beyond all expectations". Royalist hopes of drawing Parliamentary forces south, thus relieving pressure in the north, were gone.

Cheriton today:

Cheriton is seven miles out of Winchester on the A272. Turn left in the village and, after the river Itchen, take a small road to your right. Cross over two farm tracks and you come to a Y junction. There is a monument on the side of the road just beyond. The lane at the foot of the hill by the metal barn leads to Hinton Ampner, where Waller had his headquarters.

CROPREDY BRIDGE, 29th June, 1644

Oxfordshire O/S Landranger 151 (470 465)

In May 1644 the Royalist garrison at Abingdon was withdrawn to strengthen the King's army, depleted by Hopton's defeat at Cheriton and by Prince Maurice's army besieging Lyme. The Parliamentary commanders were not slow to act. Essex soon captured Abingdon, Waller guarded the Thames at Newbridge on the road between Witney and Abingdon, Massey moved on Tewkesbury, and to the north there were Roundheads at Eynsham, Woodstock and Bletchingdon. Oxford was surrounded and Charles, advised by the aged Earl of Forth, decided to act. With 5,000 horse and 2,500 infantry he left Oxford in the evening of 3rd June, passing near the Trout Inn at Godstow, crossing the river Evenlode at Church Hanborough and arriving at Bourton-on-the-Water the following day. Essex and Waller followed at a distance until they reached Stow-on-the-Wold, when for some strange reason Essex decided to march to the relief of Lyme leaving Waller to attack the King.

Charles chose this moment to return to Oxford. At Woodstock he doubled his infantry and collected some guns. To Rupert in Shrewsbury he sent a message to relieve York or if "for want of powder" this was impossible, "to march with your whole strength to Worcester to assist me". After marching to Buckingham, Charles moved towards Banbury which was threatened by Waller. On 28th June there was a small skirmish at Crouch Hill near Banbury, which was held by Waller, and the following day Charles marched north towards Daventry, keeping the Cherwell river between himself and Waller. Thinking that reinforcements were arriving for the enemy, Forth (lately created Earl of Brentford) sent a small detachment to hold the bridge at Cropredy. Waller was not slow to see the gap in the Royalist forces. He sent his cavalry under Middleton across the Cherwell at Slat Mill and attacked the bridge himself with horse, foot and eleven guns. The Royalist van gave way and, reinforced by Lord Stuart's life-guards, drew up a barricade further up the river at Hays Bridge. It was Waller's turn to be caught between two forces. Lord Cleveland's horse attacked Cropredy Bridge and scattered the defenders, capturing Waller's cannon and their officer in charge, James Wemyss, who had previously been Charles's Master Gunner. With the help of Colonel Birch who held on to the bridge itself, Waller and his horse escaped, but lost many men and supplies in doing so.

The day was the King's. Waller's army disintegrated and Oxford was safe once more. Charles wrote to his queen at Exeter to arrange for the christening of his daughter, whom he had not yet seen, but whom he had heard was 'my prettiest daughter'. In July he pursued Essex into the west leaving Rupert to manage the threat to York. Rupert moved quickly and efficiently towards York and on 1st July he entered the town and the siege was raised. In high spirits although facing twice his number of infantry, he forced the Battle of Marston Moor.

Cropredy Bridge today:

Take the A423 to Coventry and five miles north of Banbury turn right to Great Bourton and Cropredy, a small village with a great number of new houses. The bridge is near a garage but it is not the original. There is a small monument erected by a bishop built into the parapet. The fields to the west are much as they must have been in 1644 but what is really surprising is the narrowness of the river. It must have been wider before the Oxford Canal was built.

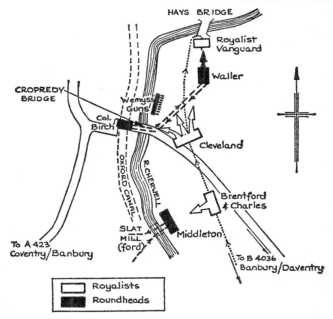

Battle of Cropredy Bridge, 1644

MARSTON MOOR, 2nd July, 1644

Yorkshire O/S Landranger 105 (491 525)

Despite Newark and a Royalist success the Scottish army in alliance with Parliament and under Lord Leven was still besieging the Marquis of Newcastle in York. Sir Thomas Fairfax and the Earl of Manchester commanded the Parliamentary troops and their total Allied force amounted to 27,000 men. Prince Rupert, with 12,000 troops arrived at Preston. On 23rd June he left for Skipton, and the alarmed Allied commanders decided to break off the siege and concentrate their forces east of York on the barren moor between the villages of Tockwith and Long Marston. On 30th June the Royalists reached Knaresborough and Rupert devised a bold plan. He sent a small cavalry squadron to make a disturbance at Tockwith and with the rest of his army he left early on 1st July for Boroughbridge. Crossing the river Ure he made for Thornton bridge over the Swale near Brafferton and turning south-east headed for York protected from the enemy by the Ouse. At Nether Poppleton he surprised some dragoons guarding a pontoon bridge and crossing his third river, arrived on the outskirts of York. The Marquis sent a letter of congratulations via Lord Goring, who had gone on ahead. Elated by his initial success, Rupert ordered an attack the following day.

"The Prince had done his work," wrote Clarendon, "and if he had sat still the other great army would have mouldered." The Scots and English on the moor were running short of water. The men squabbled with each other and discipline in the Scots army was poor. Lord Leven ordered the foot to march south to hold the bridge at Tadcaster and when Rupert arrived at Long Marston he was without his infantry because they were plundering the abandoned siege lines. Lord Eythin, who was second in command of the Whitecoats, as Newcastle's troops were known because of their undyed serge jackets (they vowed to dye them in the blood of the enemy), had been with Rupert at Lemgo in Germany where he had failed to prevent the Prince from being taken prisoner. Now his late arrival had prevented an attack that would have caught the Allies at a disadvantage.

By four in the afternoon the positions were ready. Rupert's own cavalry faced Cromwell's horse for the first time. Lord Goring faced Thomas Fairfax on the Marston wing and the foot, as at Edgehill, were in the centre. Between the two armies was a ditch lined by Royalist musketeers. On the Allied left wing the ditch was partially filled in so Cromwell's cavalry had an advantageous position. At half past seven the weather changed, and when the Royalist commanders were eating their supper, simultaneous with a clap of thunder the whole Allied line advanced.

Marston Moor was a very confused battle. Manchester's chaplain, Simon Ash, standing at the group of trees still known as Cromwell's Plump saw only 'so many thick clouds'. Byron, commanding the front line of Rupert's cavalry, was forced back but one of his officers, Colonel Trevor, hit out with his sword and caught Cromwell at the back of his neck forcing the Parliamentary leader to retire to have his wound dressed. Leslie, in charge of the second line of Parliamentary cavalry, attacked Rupert's horse in the flank and after a brief fight the Royalists were driven off the field. On the other wing Fairfax had been sharply dealt with both

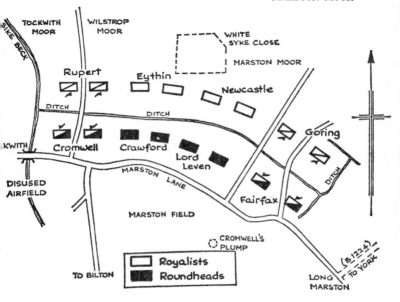

Battle of Marston Moor, 1644

by musketeers and gorse bushes. His troops were soon forced
back by Goring but he himself, wounded in the face, went
on to attempt to circle the rear of the Royalist position and
join up with Cromwell. In spite of losing his horse he
succeeded in this manoeuvre, pretending to be a Royalist
by removing his white hat band.

Cromwell returned to the fray and, stirred on by the angry
words of Lawrence Crawford, who commanded Manchester's
foot, he joined Fairfax and attacked Goring, who had to turn
about to meet his enemy. The whole line had now moved
round clockwise so that Newcastle was nearly surrounded.
"The runaways were so many . . . both armies being mingled,
horses and foot, no side keeping their own posts," wrote an
observer. Scots were flying on one side and Royalists on the
other. Cromwell's final third charge won the day and the
Whitecoats, whose leader had left them to their fate in
White Syke Close, fought to the bitter end. The total dead
was 4,000 Royalists and about 1,000 Allies. Prince Rupert,
who had been forced to hide in a beanfield to escape the

final rout, took the Royalist stragglers to Chester. York surrendered on 16th July and the Marquis of Newcastle fled to Holland to take no further part in the Civil War. A model of the battle and Civil War arms can be seen in York Museum.

Marston Moor today:

Take the B1224 from York towards Wetherby. The monument is on the right after Long Marston. On the left is Cromwell's Plump which can be reached by a footpath. There is a fine view of the battlefield from here.

LOSTWITHIEL, 2nd September, 1644

Landranger 200 (105 597)

After the victory at Cropredy Bridge, Charles led his army into Devon. Essex had relieved Plymouth, which had been besieged by Sir Richard Grenville and his small army of Cornish foot. The two western counties were predominantly Royalist and Charles's army soon swelled to about 16,000. On 7th August Essex at Lostwithiel was surrounded and Charles summoned him to surrender.

Essex was in a difficult position, but he had managed to keep open his supply line with Plymouth and the navy was under Parliamentary control. He felt safe enough to refuse the summons, but events rapidly moved against him. On 14th August a force of 2,000 under Middleton sent by Parliament to relieve him was defeated near Bridgwater by Sir Francis Doddington.

Charles made his headquarters at Boconnoc, a small village between Liskeard and Lostwithiel, and all around his army closed in on Essex's 10,000 hungry men. Grenville occupied Bodmin then stormed Restormel Castle, which the defenders gave up with little resistance. Prince Maurice, who had been besieging Lyme, and the Earl of Brentford occupied Beacon Hill and Druid's Hill on 21st August, while another Royalist troop guarded Respryn Bridge on the Fowey, thus keeping open the communications between Grenville and Charles. On 26th August Goring, who had taken over command of the cavalry from Lord Wilmot, was sent to St. Blazey to prevent Essex moving further into Cornwall. A small group of foot and guns guarded Bodinnick on the Fowey estuary. On 30th August two deserters informed Charles of Essex's plan to embark from Fowey with his infantry and send his cavalry under Balfour through the Royalist lines.

The main road from Lostwithiel to Liskeard was guarded

110

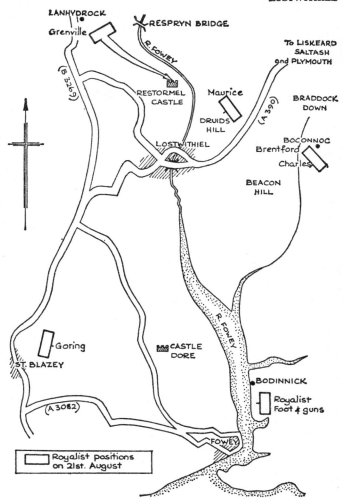

Battle of Lostwithiel, 1644

by a cottage lined with the Earl of Brentford's musketeers. At Saltash on the river Tamar the bridge was broken and Maurice's army was ordered to stand to arms all night. In spite of this at 3 a.m. Balfour's 2,000 horse escaped along the main road, beating off a force on Braddock Down. They crossed the Tamar by boat and with the loss of about 100 men they reached Plymouth before Cleveland and his cavalry could catch them. Undaunted, Charles attacked Lostwithiel The retreating Roundheads lost two large cannon in the mud together with other arms and baggage in the narrow lane to Fowey. Near Castle Dore Skippon's rearguard made a stand in the evening light. Essex's own brigade recovered some lost ground but Northampton's horse drove them back.

Essex now decided to escape. "I thought it fit to look to myself," he explained afterwards. He set sail for Plymouth in a fishing boat. After a parley on 1st September, Skippon surrendered the following day. In all, 6,000 men laid down their arms. They were too many to keep in captivity and Charles made them swear not to fight again until they reached Portsmouth, removing their arms and ammunition and capturing 42 guns. It was his greatest victory of the war.

Lostwithiel today:

The roads down to Fowey harbour are still narrow and muddy in wet weather. Lostwithiel is a charming old town, fortunately by-passed, and Fowey itself is "a haunted town made for sailors and pedestrians". The only remains of Charles's great victory that can be seen today are the earthworks at Castle Dore, near Golant, which really date from the Iron Age although they were possibly improved by the Royalists. Restormel Castle is worth a visit.

NEWBURY II, 28th October, 1644

Berkshire O/S Landranger 174 (464 685)

The two battles of Newbury are so different that the only connections between them are the antagonists and the town itself. In autumn 1644 Charles returned from his successful Lostwithiel campaign to relieve the sieges of Basing House, Donnington Castle and Banbury. On 19th October three Parliamentary armies united at Basingstoke under Essex, Waller and the Earl of Manchester. Charles's army was outnumbered by nearly two to one but, confident of his communications with Oxford, he relieved Colonel Boys's gallant

112

29. *Roundway Down, 1643: the picnic site above Bloody Ditch.*

30. *Newbury I, 1643: Bigg's Cottage where Essex stayed.*

31. Newbury I, 1643: the Falkland Monument.

32. Newbury I, 1643: the inscription on the Falkland Monument.

IN MEMORY OF THOSE
WHO ON THE 20TH SEPTEMBER 1643
FELL FIGHTING IN THE ARMY OF KING CHARLES I
ON THE FIELD OF NEWBURY: AND ESPECIALLY OF
LUCIUS CARY, VISCOUNT FALKLAND
WHO DIED HERE IN THE 34TH YEAR OF HIS AGE.
THIS MONUMENT IS SET UP BY THOSE TO WHOM
THE MAJESTY OF THE CROWN AND
THE LIBERTIES OF THEIR COUNTRY ARE DEAR.

33. Newark, 1644: Newark Castle.

34. Cheriton, 1644: the battlefield with Cheriton Wood on the right.

35. *Cropredy Bridge, 1644: the present bridge over the Cherwell.*

36. *Marston Moor, 1644: Cromwell's Plump.*

37. *Lostwithiel, 1644: the old bridge at Lostwithiel.*

38. *Newbury II, 1644: Donnington Castle.*

39. Naseby, 1645: the battle obelisk.

40. *Worcester, 1651: Powick Bridge.*

41. *Worcester, 1651: the Commandery.*

42. Sedgemoor, 1685: 'The Morning of Sedgemoor' by Edgar Bundy, painted in 1960 and now in the Tate Gallery.

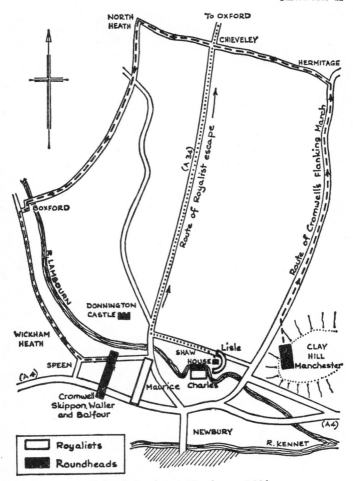

Second Battle of Newbury, 1644

force in Donnington Castle and sent the Earl of Northampton to relieve Banbury.

On 26th October the Parliamentary army was at Thatcham under the command of a council of war appointed by the

121

London Committee of Both Kingdoms. Essex was ill and Manchester was the senior officer and probably responsible for the dangerously involved plan to send Skippon, Cromwell, Waller and Balfour with almost two-thirds of the army to attack from the west. The route chosen, indicated on the map, involved a night march of thirteen miles with a bivouac at North Heath. A cannon would announce the attack and Manchester would descend from his position on Clay Hill to attack Colonel Lisle's men in Shaw House. Charles got wind of the elaborate scheme and sent Prince Maurice—whose brother Rupert was in Bath—to defend the village of Speen with his Roundway Down veterans. He himself remained in the centre with the artillery and reserve horse, his flank protected by the river Lambourn.

The weather was dull and it became dark at 5 o'clock. Skippon's weary men attacked Prince Maurice at 3 o'clock but Manchester, perhaps confused by Donnington's cannon, did not move. Lord Cleveland, who had led the charge that captured the bridge at Cropredy, saved Maurice from being overrun while Boys kept Cromwell, who was strangely subdued, at bay under the guns of Donnington Castle. When Manchester at last attacked the earthworks round Shaw House, it was so dark that Colonel Lisle had to remove his coat so his men could see his white shirt. The Roundheads were chased up Clay Hill and in the west Skippon could not get past Speen. During the night Charles withdrew to Bath and his army to Oxford. Men moved so quietly that Charles's enemies were surprised to find next morning that the town was theirs. A week later 1,500 Royalists returned, this time with Rupert, relieved the castle and recovered their artillery, while a small party under Colonel Gage relieved Basing House. There was no third battle at Newbury because Manchester had no stomach for it. "If we beat the King ninety-nine times he will be King still," he said, "but if he beat us but once for the last time, we shall be hanged."

Newbury today:

Leave Newbury by the A34 and Donnington Castle gatehouse (open free to the public) is on the hill at the far end of the village of Donnington. Retrace your steps, cross over the A34 and you come to Shaw House, now a school. Above you is Clay Hill where Manchester camped. There are no signs of the battle but it is much easier to visualise than the first battle of Newbury. In Newbury's museum are models of both battles.

NASEBY, 14th June, 1645

Northamptonshire O/S Landranger 141 (682 801)

At the beginning of 1645, Parliament had gained decisive victories in the north at Marston Moor and in the south at Cheriton. Victory against the King himself had eluded them, and the Royalists still held the south-west. After a period of drastic reorganisation in the high command, removing all who, like Manchester, were reluctant to beat the King in battle, the New Model Army under Fairfax was formed at Windsor.

In May Prince Rupert, who was now the Royalist Commander-in-Chief, attacked and captured Leicester while Fairfax and the New Model Army besieged Oxford. Moving south, some of Charles's vanguard were captured at an inn in the village of Naseby. Charles called a council during the night and early next morning Rupert, who had wanted to join forces with Goring's cavalry in the west before fighting, moved forward towards Naseby, finding on Dust Hill an ideal position to line up his troops with the wind behind them to blow smoke into the enemy. It was time to avenge Marston Moor.

The New Model Army, greatly superior in numbers, had also found a ridge on which to form their line of battle. Cromwell's three lines of cavalry were on the right facing Langdale's Northern Horse; Skippon, the veteran of Newbury, 1643, was in the centre with the infantry and opposite Astley and Charles, while on the right stood Ireton's horse facing Rupert and Maurice. The start of the battle was Edgehill all over again. Rupert's fierce charge drove most of Ireton's horse off the field and only the musketeers round the baggage train behind forced the Cavaliers back. Astley's infantry advanced on Skippon, who was wounded, but they in turn were charged by Ireton himself with a troop of horse that had not fled from Rupert, and also by Okey's dragoons. Ireton was captured and, if it had not been for Cromwell, Charles might have carried off an overwhelming victory.

Cromwell's first troop under Whalley advanced on Langdale, whose inferior horsemen were driven off the field. Cromwell himself charged with his own troop in a left wheel on the flank of Astley's infantry. Charles, trying to intervene with his reserve, was forestalled by the Earl of Carnwarth who seized his rein and shouted: "Will you go upon your death?" Rupert, returning, realised the situation was hopeless and fled with the King to Leicester and Ashby-de-la-Zouch Castle.

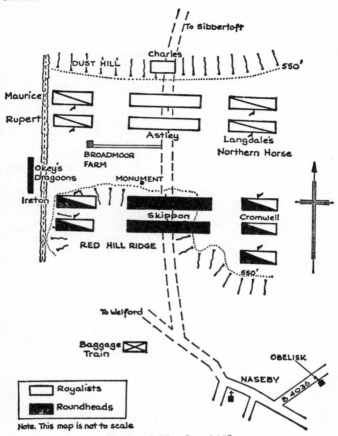

Battle of Naseby, 1645

Astley's men laid down their arms. Only Rupert's Bluecoats fought to the bitter end. By lunch time the battle was over. Fairfax had captured the Royal baggage, which included all Charles's correspondence and about £100,000 in gold, silver and jewels. Some 4,000 cavalry remained to the King but all Astley's foot had either been killed, wounded or captured. On 17th June Leicester surrendered to Fairfax. Cromwell who closed his eyes to the slaughter of some 200 women camp followers on "grounds of moral principle", could well declare that Naseby was a victory "Of which I had great assurance and God did it".

The King's cause was lost and he finally gave himself up to the Scots in May 1646, a year in which only Montrose in Scotland and the north was to see success for the Royalists

Naseby today:
Between Northampton and Market Harborough off the A50, Naseby village is 600 feet high and close to the source of the Avon. Take the Welford road north-west from Naseby turning right to Sibbertoft almost immediately. The first ridge marks the Round-head position and there is a monument. It was put up in 1936, supposedly, but incorrectly, showing the starting point of Cromwell's charge. Broadmoor farm below is near where Rupert charged. The Royalist slope is not so steep. A battle museum is behind the garage in the village. An obelisk on the B4036 near Naseby village put up in 1823 by the lord of the manor, states that the battle: "led to the subversion of the throne, the altar and the constitution ... leaving a useful lesson to British kings never to exceed the bounds of their prerogative."

The new A1/M1 link road will go through the site of the battle close to the Parliamentary Baggage Train.

LANGPORT, 10th July, 1645

Somerset O/S Landranger 193 (441 271)

The Battle of Naseby did not end Royalist hopes, for Lord Goring was in Somerset besieging Taunton with an undefeated army of about 7,000 men. Fairfax, after capturing Leicester, decided to relieve Taunton, where Blake was holding out against the Royalists. Marching via Stonehenge and Dorchester he forced Goring to abandon his positions and form up on the river Yeo near Yeovil, taking care to destroy all the bridges on a twelve-mile front.

On the night of 7th July the Parliamentary infantry crossed the river at Yeovil and Goring was forced back to Langport. On the 9th Goring decided on a rush to divide the enemy's strength and he sent his cavalry under Porter, his brother-in-law, in the direction of Bridgwater and Taunton. Fairfax detached Massey and nearly 4,000 horse in pursuit. There was a skirmish near Ilminster and some of the Cavalier horse were captured. Porter withdrew hastily and Goring had to come out of Langport to beat back the Parliamentary horse.

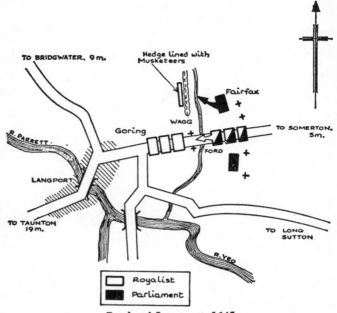

Battle of Langport, 1645

The Royalists now decided to fall back on Bridgwater and on the 10th their artillery departed while Goring took up a defensive position at Langport near the hamlet of Wagg. He had returned two guns to guard the road from Fairfax's headquarters at Long Sutton. Musketeers were posted along the hedge and the river Yeo was protected on the right. It was a fairly strong position as the Parliamentary advance would have to advance four abreast and cross a ford to get to him.

Fairfax concentrated his artillery on the two guns, which were soon silenced. He then sent in his musketeers to attack the Royalist musketeers and when this succeeded three troops of horse under Major Bethel charged across the ford and into the Royalist horse and infantry, arranged in three lines. Desborough's horse came to the aid of Bethel and on the other flank the musketeers fired on the Royalists.

Fairfax advanced and the Royalist foot surrendered, the cavalry escaping to Bridgwater which surrendered on 23rd

July after a struggle. Apart from Rupert at Bristol, western Royalists had virtually ceased to exist and the end was not far away.

Langport today:

The battlefield is best viewed from the top of Huish Episcopi church. The Royalists were defending the Wagg Rhyne and the slope up from the direction of Somerton is the route taken by Bethel. Fairfax's musketeers must have arrived at just the right time to win the day for Massey's cavalry had rejoined Fairfax after their skirmish at Ilminster. Wagg bridge, which replaced the ford, is a few miles out of Langport on the Somerton road B3153.

ROWTON HEATH, 24th September, 1645

Cheshire O/S Landranger 117 (445 645)

Parliament gained virtual control of the north at Marston Moor, but in September Charles scored a great victory at Lostwithiel. Returning, he had to face three Parliamentary armies at Reading, and although beaten, managed to escape with most of his army to Oxford. At the beginning of 1645 abortive peace talks were held and Parliament proceeded to organise the New Model Army, which succeeded in preventing Prince Rupert from gathering his forces to invade Lancashire and Yorkshire. In June the great defeat at Naseby in Northants resulted in the annihilation of the King's army—he was never again able to muster so many. Further Roundhead successes followed fast and the last hopes of Charles were now centred on the Highlanders of James Graham, Earl of Montrose, but he, having made himself master of Scotland by his victories in 1644 and 1645 was defeated at Philiphaugh on 13th September 1645.

After Naseby, King Charles had only his cavalry in the north to defend him from the New Model Army. Goring was defeated at Langport in Somerset on 10th July and Prince Rupert surrendered Bristol to Fairfax and was deprived of his commission by the King. The Parliamentary commander in the north was Colonel-General Poyntz, a professional soldier recently returned from overseas, whose troop of dragoons numbered 3,000, about the size of the King's remaining cavalry.

Travelling from South Wales via Worcester and Denbigh castle Charles arrived in Chester on 23rd September, hotly pursued by Poyntz. Langdale was sent over the river Dee at Holt, where the Royalists had constructed a bridge of boats, to attack Poyntz and the army besieging Chester in the rear. At 9.00 a.m. Langdale, who knew Poyntz's plans from an intercepted letter, charged the Parliamentarians in the flank and drove them off with loss. Poyntz rallied his men and managed to take up a position on Hatton Down near Rowton, where he was in touch with the besiegers who strengthened his force with 300 foot under Lothian and 500 horse under Colonel Jones.

Charles in Chester had sent out a relieving force under Lord Bernard Stuart, by then the Earl of Lichfield, and Lord Gerard. Before they could join with Langdale, Poyntz attacked. His charge drove Langdale back to Chester's walls where Gerard and Lichfield stemmed the retreat. "But the disorder of those horse which first fled," explains Clarendon, "had so filled the narrow ways that at last the enemy's musketeers compelled the King's horse to turn and to rout one another and to overbear their own officers who would have restrained them." The shrewd Poyntz had succeeded in drawing out the cavalry into territory unsuitable for horses, for although Rowton is flat, the narrow lanes nearer to Chester were ideal for musketeers and the main battle was fought there rather than at Rowton. Charles, who had seen the battle from the city walls, fell back to Denbigh leaving behind 800 prisoners and 600 wounded and dead. Among the latter was Charles's cousin, the gallant Earl of Lichfield, who in 1642 had begged permission from Charles to fight with Prince Rupert at the first main battle of the Civil War—Edgehill. His cause lost, Charles finally gave himself up to the Scots in May 1646.

Rowton Heath today:

About three miles south-east of Chester on the A41, Rowton is a suburb of Chester but still retains a few green fields. The modern 'Ye Old Trooper Inn' by the canal bridge is the only thing to remind one of the battle. It seems inconceivable that the King could have seen the action from the city walls. It is more likely that he saw the later rout under the walls, some of which still stand today. There is no monument.

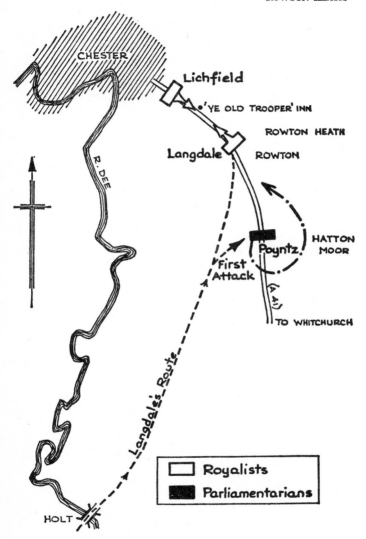

Battle of Rowton Heath, 1645

PRESTON, 17th-18th August, 1648
Lancashire O/S Landranger 102 (551 321)

After the defeat of Montrose in 1645 the Royalist power in Scotland passed to the Duke of Hamilton, who was a moderate Presbyterian with many friends in England. When the Second Civil War broke out in May 1648 in Wales, Cromwell immediately set forth for Pembroke sending General Lambert to Yorkshire where Scarborough and Pontefract castles had been seized by Royalists. Charles was a prisoner in the Isle of Wight but he had signed a document known as the Engagement agreeing to a Scottish invasion.

Hamilton, supported by his brother the Earl of Lanark and the Earl of Callendar, raised an army of 10,000 and crossed the border on 8th July intending to make for Wales where, unknown to him, the rebellion had already fizzled out. Cromwell joined Lambert at Knaresborough. They had 'a fine smart army fit for action' of about 8,500. Hamilton had been reinforced by 3,000 men under Sir Marmaduke Langdale, who was the Royalist leader at Rowton Heath. Another Royalist army, small but well armed, landed in Galloway from Ulster under Sir George Monro. On 16th August the Parliamentarians camped in Stonyhurst Park. Langdale, who was leading the vanguard, spotted them and sent to Hamilton for reinforcements which never materialised. The Scottish cavalry under Middleton was far to the south at Wigan and the infantry were preparing to cross the Ribble when Cromwell attacked. Langdale had placed his troops on a bank overlooking Ribbleton Moor. They checked the oncoming troopers and fought them from hedge to hedge. One detachment of Cromwell's horse reached the bridge before Langdale and only with difficulty did the cavaliers escape leaving many dead and several hundred prisoners in the town. Hamilton personally led his own regiment of horse to beat off the Roundheads from the bridge. By crossing at a ford over the Ribble he managed to rejoin the infantry, who had been drawn up on the banks of the Darwen at Walton.

The night was so wet that the Royalist leaders decided to march on to Wigan and join up with Middleton. They marched swiftly and all the powder wagons were left behind. The orders for them to be blown up were never carried out and Cromwell, who had already captured Hamilton's personal plate, now captured his army's powder. The Royalist

130

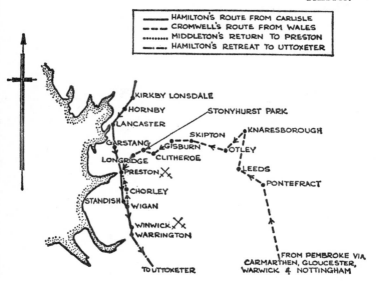

The Northern Campaign, 1648

cavalry had decided to join up with their foot and the two passed each other at night and Middleton, a former Round-head, found Cromwell not Hamilton at Walton. The presence of Monro, who was moving slowly south through the Lake District, meant Cromwell had to leave part of his force behind in Preston. Meanwhile Colonel Thornhaugh, pursuing Middleton, was cut off and killed. It was the one Royalist success of the campaign.

On 18th August the Scots, tired, hungry and depressed by the continual retreat, turned at Winwick, where there was a natural defile, and held up Cromwell for three hours. At least a thousand Scots were killed and many fled to the church where they were captured. Baillie and 2,600 Scottish infantry surrendered in Warrington and only Hamilton an the remaining cavalry carried on south to surrender on 25th August at Uttoxeter. Hamilton was later executed in London. The Earl of Lanark refused to let the English leaders take refuge in Scotland and many were captured. Monro and most of his army returned to Ulster. Colonel Turner, one of the English Royalists, summed up the defeat: "The

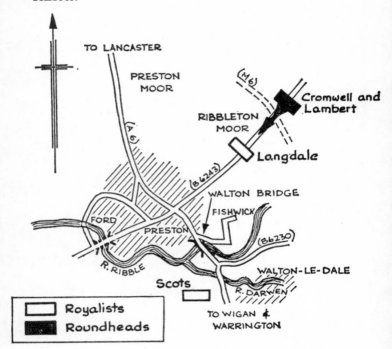

Battle of Preston, 1648

weakness, rawness and undisciplinedness of our troops, our
want of artillery and horse ... made us a prey to Cromwell's
army. What was intended for the King's relief and restoration
posted him to his grave."

Preston today:

The town rises high above the Ribble and the bridge must
have been difficult to capture. There is a dramatic picture
of the battle in the Harris Museum in the Market Square.
Below this are three swords, two of which belong to the
second battle of Preston in 1715 which was a surrender
rather than a battle. Winwick is just off the M6 (exit 22) and
the present church is Victorian. The only monument is a
plaque on the Unicorn Cafe near Walton bridge.

WORCESTER, 3rd September, 1651
Worcestershire O/S Landranger 150 (846 525)

In August 1651 young Charles, who had been proclaimed King Charles II at Scone, crossed into England with a Scottish army of nearly 17,000 men under Hamilton and Leslie. It was a formidable force and General Lambert hurrying north with his cavalry to Warrington was quickly sent flying south to Coventry. On 22nd August, having advanced via Newport and Wolverhampton, Charles arrived at Worcester.

The Scots had pillaged on their march and few English Royalists joined them. (Ninety-four years later Prince Charles discovered the same thing and his army was smaller than the

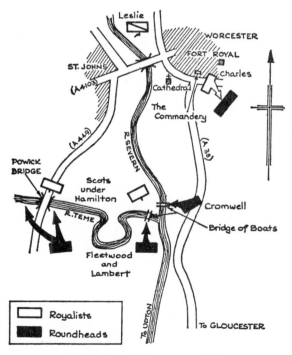

Battle of Worcester, 1651

Royalists' at Worcester.) Cromwell collected an army of about 28,000 and moved towards Worcester from Nottingham. Lambert seized the Severn bridge at Upton and Charles's only remaining escape route was to the north. Charles hastily organised the defences of Worcester, relying on the Severn and the Teme which meet near Powick Bridge to protect him from Lambert, and Fort Royal with its guns to protect him from Cromwell. Leslie's horse were positioned outside the gates to the north.

Fleetwood's garrison from Banbury had now arrived at Upton and Cromwell placed him in charge of the western bank of the Severn. Twenty boats were assembled to act as a bridge which would be floated upstream to form bridges across both Teme and Severn. It was a bold plan and it succeeded under the noses of the Scottish infantry who were thrown off balance by a troop of horse that crossed by a ford south of Powick Bridge. Fierce fighting took place here, the spot where Rupert had won his cavalry battle in September 1642. It was also the anniversary of Cromwell's great victory over the Scots at Dunbar, which discouraged Leslie from fighting at all.

Charles, watching from the cathedral tower, possibly saw bridges quickly assembled and Cromwell cross with his regiment to consult Lambert and Fleetwood. Noticing that the Roundhead right wing was now leaderless and isolated, the young prince gathered all the troops he could find and charged out of the east gate, protected by the guns of Fort Royal. The Roundheads reeled in surprise and a cavalry charge would have routed them but Leslie still would not move. In spite of all Charles's pleas the Scottish cavalry fled by the road to the north. Cromwell's reappearance on the right wing in the nick of time had proved his greatness as a general. His regiment forced the Royalists back into the town where many were killed in the narrow streets. It was "his crowning mercy" and one of his greatest victories.

One thing marred Cromwell's victory. In the evening light —the battle had lasted fully five hours and the bridges were not complete until mid-afternoon—Charles escaped with one or two faithful followers to the safety of the Giffords at Whiteladies and Boscobel and ultimately across the Channel.

Worcester today:

There is little to see of the battlefield of Worcester because it was not a field battle. Old Powick Bridge still stands although partially rebuilt in 1837. It is now used mostly by fishermen. One can walk along the banks to the junction of the Teme and the Severn and see where the bridges of boats were erected. The house where Charles escaped is still standing in New Street. The Marquis of Hamilton's monument is in the Cathedral; he was mortally wounded in the last desperate sally from the narrow Commandery cobbled alley which remains much as it must have looked in 1651. The Commandery has an audio-visual show about the battle and a small museum.

SEDGEMOOR, 6th July, 1685
Somerset O/S Landranger 182 (355 361)

In June 1685 the Duke of Monmouth, natural son of Charles II, landed at Lyme with a handful of supporters, declaring his uncle James II, who had been king for only four months, to be a usurper, and claiming the throne for himself. The West Country puritans, who had cheered the Duke on his tour several years before, responded to his call and an army of about 4,000 men was assembled which included 800 horse under Lord Grey and four cannon under Dutch gunners. The King's army was commanded by a Frenchman, Lord Feversham, but its second-in-command was John Churchill, future Duke of Marlborough, and two of its regiments were the redoubtable Kirke's Lambs newly returned from Tangier.

After failing to capture Bristol but defeating a Royal force at Norton St. Philip, Monmouth camped in Bridgwater on 3rd July. Feversham followed at a distance, slowed down by his seventeen cannon, and reached Weston Zoyland on 5th July. An outpost of royal cavalry under Sir Francis Compton occupied the village of Chedzoy and another under General Oglethorpe occupied Bawdrip. The cannon covered the Bridgwater road so Monmouth had either to attack or retreat.

He decided on a night attack and the weather helped him for it was foggy as well as very dark. A local guide, Godfrey, led his army in a long narrow column out of Bridgwater on the Bristol road until they turned right to Peasey Farm, where the ammunition carts were left. Both of Feversham's outposts were avoided, by luck rather than judgement, and the Langmoor Rhine, a ditch of some seventeen feet in width, was being crossed when a shot rang out. The rebels were discovered and Grey's horse promptly attacked in an attempt to get round to the rear of Feversham's forces, while the infantry attacked the front. It was a bold move but Bussex Rhine, another deep ditch a mile away, prevented it. James's army

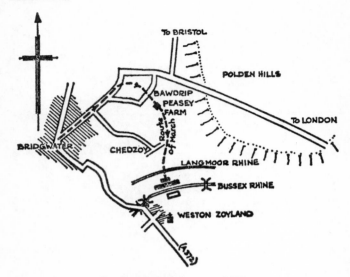

SEDGEMOOR

TO BRISTOL

POLDEN HILLS

BAWDRIP

PEASEY FARM

TO LONDON

Route of March

BRIDGWATER

CHEDZOY

LANGMOOR RHINE

BUSSEX RHINE

WESTON ZOYLAND

(A372)

Battle of Sedgemoor, 1685
Monmouth's route from Bridgwater (above)
and the plan of battle (below)

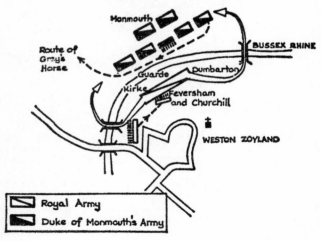

Monmouth

Route of Grey's Horse

BUSSEX RHINE

Guards

Dumbarton

Kirke

Feversham and Churchill

WESTON ZOYLAND

Royal Army

Duke of Monmouth's Army

lined one side and the rebels the other. A firing battle went on all night, the rebel artillery taking toll of the Dumbarton's Brigade and the Guards, until it ran out of ammunition. Meanwhile Grey's inexperienced horse had galloped across the enemy front and disappeared until the end of the battle, which came with the daylight. The Bishop of Winchester, a former soldier who was an interested spectator, lent his horses to the frustrated Royal gunners and six guns bore down on the unfortunate rebels, deciding the day.

Monmouth, Grey and a few others escaped to the Polden Hills and the infantry, mostly armed with scythes and bill-hooks, were rounded up or killed on the moor by Kirke's Lambs. Monmouth was later captured and executed but Grey was pardoned, despite Jeffreys' Bloody Assizes.

Sedgemoor today:

Take the A303 from Wincanton until it becomes the A372. Before Bridgwater turn right at Weston Zoyland. Follow signs to the battlefield. It is confusing because the Bussex Rhine no longer exists and the ditch you see is modern. There is an interpretation board by Bussex Farm and an excellent model of the battle in the Admiral Blake Museum, Bridgwater.

CLIFTON MOOR, 18th December, 1745
Westmorland O/S Landranger 90 (532 269)

The Jacobites retreated from Derby on 6th December. It was a disastrous step for their morale but, in the circumstances, a wise one. General Wade was in a position to cut them off on the border and the Duke of Cumberland with 4,000 dragoons and about 3,000 infantry blocked the road at Lichfield.

The retreat was a difficult business due to the state of the roads in winter and the slowness of the artillery and baggage. On 18th December Charles arrived at Penrith but the artillery and rearguard were six miles behind at Clifton, a small village on a slight hill. A collection of local militia, poorly armed but mounted, suddenly appeared on the road between Penrith and Clifton. Lord George Murray, commanding the rearguard, which consisted of Macdonald of Glengarry's Regiment, charged them and captured two men, one of whom was the Duke of Cumberland's servant. The latter informed Lord George that the Duke and 4,000 men were hot on his heels, so a further three regiments, Cluny's MacPhersons, Colonel Roy Stewart's men and the Stewarts of Appin were marched back to Clifton where Lord George posted them behind the enclosed walls of the village. The artillery was sent on to Penrith and at 4 o'clock the dragoons appeared, about 500 of them dismounted in two lines making for the enclosures. The Duke had sent forward ten men from each platoon.

Lord George sent Cluny's men up to a thick hedge which they burst through and they fell on the dragoons. The latter had time to fire once before the Jacobites led by Lord George, by now hatless and wigless, were on them. About twelve dragoons were killed and many wounded. The MacPhersons broke fourteen swords on the metal skull caps of the Englishmen. 'We did very well,' said one Highlander after the fight, 'until the lang man in muckle boots came over the dyke.' This was Colonel Honeywood, Commander of Bland's Regiment (later the Queen's Own Hussars). He was badly wounded but recovered. He was later promoted to General of Horse. His sword and those of the fallen were eagerly picked up by Cluny MacPherson's men.

Meanwhile the Glengarry Regiment had been positioned behind a stone wall overlooking the road with the small regiment of Colonel Roy Stewart behind them as a rearguard. When a party of dragoons tried to take Cluny on the flank they drove them off by their brisk fire. The white belts of the dragoons shone in the moonlight but soon it was so dark that it became difficult to tell friend from foe.

The dragoons retreated leaving ten dead and many wounded including the gallant Colonel Honeywood. About four of Cluny's men were killed and about twelve captured because they pursued too far and ran into the main body of Cumberland's men drawn up on the moor. These prisoners were very unfortunate. Taken to York, a few were executed and others were sold as slaves to America. One of the latter returned to France and became a sergeant in the Regiment of Royal Scots.

The skirmish, for it was hardly a battle, was a triumph for Lord George Murray and the Prince's aide-de-camp Colonel Ker. The Prince had given orders for them to retreat rather than risk action, but Lord George had disobeyed them to beat off the pursuit. The Duke of Perth who had informed Charles personally of the presence of the dragoons had sent the Atholl Regiment with some of his own men to

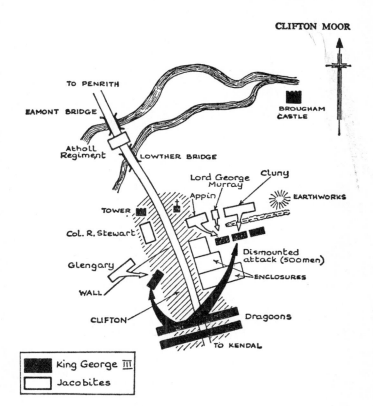

Battle of Clifton Moor, 1745

Lowther bridge under the Count of Nairne as a reinforcement, but they were never used.

Clifton Moor today:

The village of Clifton lies six miles south of Penrith on the A6. The little church has a monument, recently erected by the Queen's Own Hussars, to the men of Bland's Regiment. The tower on the other side of the church, which might have been used as a strongpoint during the fight, can be visited with permission from the farmer. At Towend Farm there is an oak tree with a small monument to two Highlanders killed when they were cut off in the attack.

INDEX